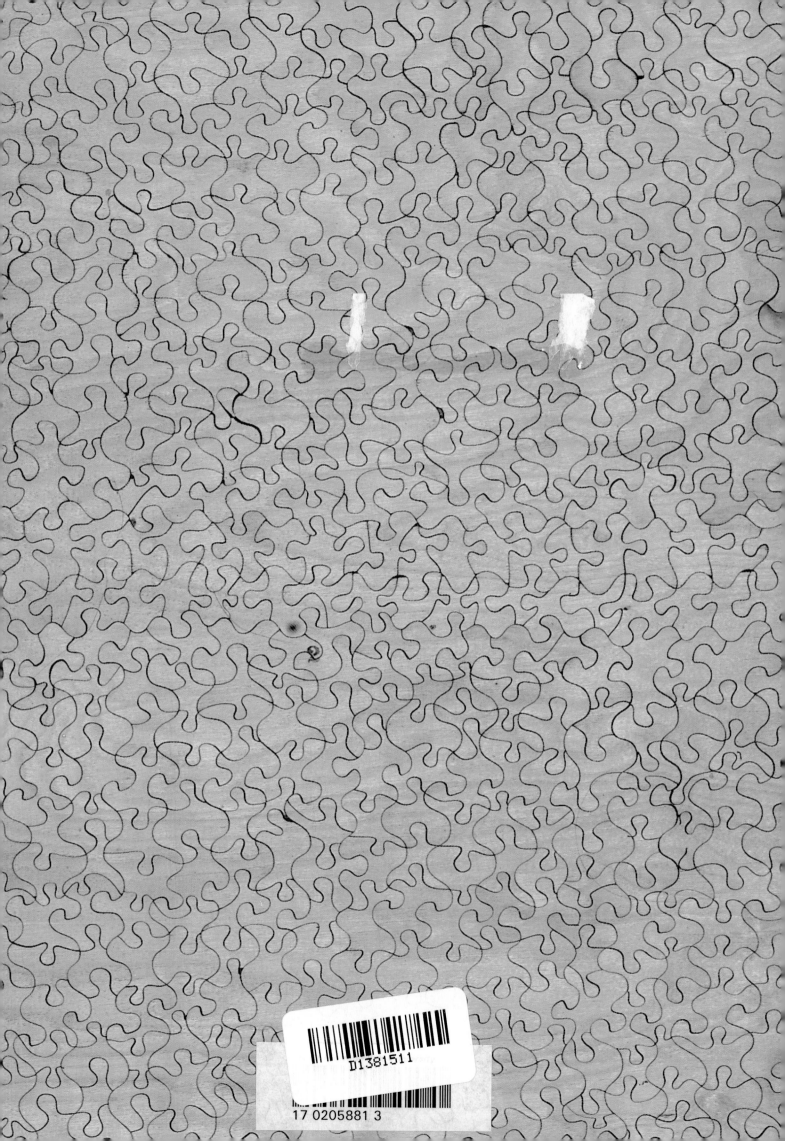

BRITISH JIGSAW PUZZLES OF THE TWENTIETH CENTURY

To my mother who introduced me to
jigsaw puzzles and who, at the age of
ninety five, helped me to assemble
puzzles for this book.

The art of the jigsaw lies in the talent of the cutter.

Gathering Flowers by
Miss K. M. Briscoe.

BRITISH JIGSAW PUZZLES OF THE TWENTIETH CENTURY

Tom Tyler

RICHARD DENNIS
1997

ACKNOWLEDGEMENTS

It is difficult to know where to begin because I owe thanks to so many. First to my publisher, Richard Dennis, who suggested I should write this book and, in addition to loaning me puzzles from his collection, has given me unfailing support and advice throughout. My thanks to his staff, Wendy and Sue, and the team at Flaydemouse, who have enabled the whole idea to become a reality.

I have had invaluable help from members of the Benevolent Confraternity of Dissectologists. Michael Foster has given me advice and access to his considerable archive material. Kevin Holmes allowed me access to his archives and loaned important puzzles. Dave and Val Cooper have given much information and loaned a wealth of superb puzzles from their large and cherished collection. Brian Price provided his research on Victory puzzles and he and Jill have not only lent exciting puzzles from their collection but helped us to photograph them. B.C.D. members have been most generous and trusting in lending me many treasured puzzles and my particular thanks go to Bill and Molly Barnes, Geoff and Betty Hall, Ron and Elizabeth Kersey, George and Glad Farmer, Les Baker, John Squire and Meredith Worsfold. My thanks also to Brian Ball and John Stevenson for loaning me their puzzles.

The jigsaw puzzle industry itself has given me great support in this project. My thanks to Harry Jondorf for his invaluable assistance on the histories of Tower Press, Arrow Games and Falcon Games. Thanks too for the helpful information, catalogues and sample jigsaw puzzles from Cheatwell Games (Eleanor Kendall); Cranham Publications (Andrew Gillett); Falcon Games (Emily Jones); Gee Graphics (Colin Gee); Gibson Games (Roger Heyworth); James Hamilton (Gordon McGee); Handley Printers (Adrian Bostock); W.R. Kelly (Tony Baker); Robert Longstaff; George Luck; Mandolin Puzzles (Lalage Waldman); Moat House Products (Peter Tuck); Optimago; Orchard Toys (Julia Sherrington); Pentaplex; Ravensburger (Harald Pfanner); Really Useful Games; Seddons Printing and Packaging (Richard Seddon); Peter and Jonathan Stocken; Tomahawk Toys; John and Tony Trowsdale; John Waddington (Valerie Rushworth and many other staff); and the Wentworth Wooden Jigsaw Co. Ltd. (Kevin Preston and his staff).

I have had enormous help in actually assembling the puzzles to be photographed, some of which took as many thirty-six man/woman hours. In particular I wish to thank Ken Nugent, Jill Ainslie and her family, Ray and June Collins, David and Margaret Smith, Greta Berry and her family and Cecily Greaves.

My deepest thanks and gratitude to my wife and family who have helped and supported me in so many ways.

T.T.

Edited by Sue Evans
Digital photography, print, design and reproduction by Flaydemouse, Yeovil, Somerset
Published by Richard Dennis, The Old Chapel, Shepton Beauchamp, Somerset TA19 OLE, England
© 1997 Richard Dennis & Tom Tyler
ISBN 0 903685 56 6

Front cover: *The Mock Turtle's Story* from *Alice in Wonderland*. Cut by Vera Tassell and Helen Helmore, 900 pieces, wooden, c.1925.
Back cover: *Soldier Carousing*. Maker unknown, retailed by Selfridges and Co. Ltd., 200 pieces, wooden, c.1910.

CONTENTS

FOREWORD   6

INTRODUCTION   7

CHAPTER 1
Background – The Period up to 1900   9

CHAPTER 2
A Relevant Social History of the Twentieth Century   13

CHAPTER 3
Technical Developments in the Twentieth Century   16

CHAPTER 4
Commercial Pressures and Influence, Rarity and Prices   23

CHAPTER 5
Histories of Representative Twentieth-Century Jigsaw
Puzzle Manufacturers   26

CHAPTER 6
The Amateur Jigsaw Puzzle Maker   37

CHAPTER 7
Jigsaw Libraries, Clubs and Societies   39

CHAPTER 8
British Jigsaw Puzzles in the Year 2000   42

COLOUR PLATES   45

CHAPTER 9
Twentieth-Century British Jigsaw Puzzle Manufacturers   125

BIBLIOGRAPHY   131

INDEX   131

FOREWORD

Jigsaws are fun. From my childhood on, I have spent countless hours happily doing them. Forty years ago, before the age of television, jigsaws were one of the ways you could pass a wet and cold afternoon or evening and there was an enormous variety to choose from. In the 1940s I remember doing the circular puzzles from Waddington's – one had scenes from *The Yeoman of the Guard*, another different types of transport, and another various pieces of equipment used in air-raids like search-lights and barrage balloons. Then there were puzzles, in yellow and red boxes, of scenes from famous films. In those days films were very special events and I remember, in particular, scenes from *The Prisoner of Zenda* with Ronald Coleman and *Robin Hood* with Errol Flynn. A little more up-market, were the wooden puzzles, with long thin pieces, produced by the Great Western Railway of scenes from towns which their trains passed through, like Stratford-upon-Avon and the West Country.

That period was perhaps the twilight of the 'Golden Age of the Jigsaw'. It started with the ingenious wooden jigsaws of the early years of the century which continued into the 1920s and 1930s. These were beautifully cut and designed to confuse and deceive – just like the one on the cover of this book. Some of my favourite jigsaws come from this period.

The period just after the Second World War was a little bleak because there was a restriction on the use of paper. Most of the jigsaw puzzle makers seemed to concentrate on producing puzzles with pieces of exactly the same shape, and sometimes the same colour. Thankfully, that has all changed and there is now a huge variety of pictures – landscapes, famous paintings, battles, infuriating scenes of endless sky and – happily – different shaped pieces have been re-introduced and there are even vertical and three-dimensional puzzles. The first jigsaws were educational with maps of Great Britain, alphabets and kings and queens, and today's children can still learn a lot from them for some are specifically designed to convey information.

We are particularly lucky that in Doncaster, Peter Stocken and his sons cut wooden jigsaws into wonderfully ingenious shapes. They are unique and test one's patience to the ultimate.

Doing a jigsaw is not a solitary pursuit and people of all ages still enjoy them. At Christmas this year, we will have a table with a large jigsaw set out on it so that anybody in the family can add a piece when they want.

Lord Baker of Dorking, CH
September, 1997

INTRODUCTION

In 1972 Linda Hannas published her book *The English Jigsaw Puzzle 1760-1890* and this book is intended to be the sequel to her work. Jigsaw puzzle enthusiasts are immensely indebted to Linda for her detailed research on the earlier period and, in particular, her discovery that John Spilsbury was the true inventor of the jigsaw puzzle. In the first chapter of this book I have drawn extensively on Linda's work in order to set the scene for this second part of the story covering the twentieth century.

Jigsaw puzzles have been a source of amusement, challenge and fellowship for nearly two hundred and fifty years, yet the research into their history has really only taken place over the last thirty years coinciding with the increase in collections of puzzles and their often painstaking restoration. This book is for all those who enjoy jigsaw puzzles. Some will be serious collectors and restorers, well versed in the research on the subject. For such, I hope the book will provide a comprehensive survey of the subject during the century and if the book gives rise to further research and publications in the future, I shall be delighted. Those who simply enjoy the challenge of jigsaw puzzles, who relish the battle of wits between maker and assembler which is at the very heart of the hobby will, I hope, find this book informative and interesting, and an encouragement to their hobby.

Readers will be aware of the immense help I have received from so many people. This is really a joint effort by our B.C.D. Jigsaw Puzzle Club and, while I have named many individual members, much credit should go to the club as a whole and the large number of friends without whom the book would never have been written. The fact that it has been such a co-operative venture has made it at all times an enjoyable task and the most fascinating and memorable experience of my life.

No single book could fully cover the enormous range of puzzles produced during this eventful century and I will be pleased to hear from anyone who can add to our existing information on a hobby which is continually growing and developing. Long may it continue to do so!

T.T.

A COMPENDIUM OF BRITISH JIGSAW PUZZLES OF THE TWENTIETH CENTURY

by Tom Tyler

A companion volume to this book listing all recorded British jigsaws manufactured this century.

To be updated with support from your good selves.

available from

Richard Dennis, The Old Chapel, Shepton Beauchamp, Somerset TA19 OLE, England
ISBN 0 903685 59 0

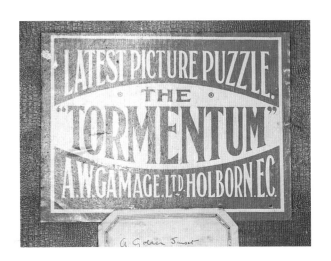

CHAPTER 1

BACKGROUND – THE PERIOD UP TO 1900

It is very difficult to take ourselves back to the year 1750. Transport was by coach, cart or boat. Steam power was beginning to be utilised, mainly for mine pumping engines, but it would be another half-century before many boats, coaches and railways engines made use of it. The windmill and watermill still supplied a great deal of power and tools were traditional and often primitive.

Education continued to be the prerogative of the richer members of society and, usually, was utilitarian and practical – equipping children to become productive adults as quickly as possible. In 1750 children as young as six were working long hours in factories, pulling carts down coal mines or being thrust up chimneys. Childhood was generally seen as an unavoidable, though ideally short, period of transition to adult status.

Publishing techniques were basic. The same methods had been in use for nearly three hundred years. A picture was etched on metal or carved on to wooden blocks and raised letters were placed in a frame, then smeared with printers ink and pressed on to a sheet of paper. Quite elaborate black-and-white prints were produced which could then be coloured by hand. In particular there was a brisk trade in maps – knowledge of the world was constantly expanding as explorers such as Captain Cook journeyed to the more distant and unknown parts of the world and combined increasingly accurate map-making with their travels.

John Spilsbury was born in Worcester in 1739 and Linda Hannas' book *The English Jigsaw Puzzle 1760-1890* gives a very detailed account of his life. He later moved to London and was, in about 1753, apprenticed to Thomas Jefferys an important map-maker and engraver. He was still with Jefferys in 1760 in his seventh year as an apprentice.

At this time there were two developments which interested John Spilsbury. There was a growing demand for children's books and the printers of the day recognised that this could constitute a specific market. At the same time John Jeffery, a printer, published a geographical race game as an aid to children's education.

During the early 1760s John Spilsbury mounted a map of England on to a thin sheet of mahogany board, used a fretsaw to cut round the county boundaries and sold the pieces, boxed, for children to assemble. Like all great inventions it was very simple. This was the first 'dissected map' or true jigsaw puzzle. It was an English invention and we can, thanks to Linda Hannas, date it with great confidence. It seems likely that the Dutch were very early

copiers of the idea – perhaps within five years or so – but it was nearly a century before the manufacture of jigsaw puzzles spread across the Atlantic. During their formative years, dissected maps and pictures were very much a European invention. Sadly, John Spilsbury died in 1769 at the early age of thirty, but his brilliant invention will surely survive in various forms.

During the next hundred years three developments took place which made John Spilsbury's idea easier to exploit commercially. Saws needed for the cutting of more intricate designs were developed and, by the end of the nineteenth century, the first treadle-operated jigsaws were produced. Primarily these were designed for cutting jigsaw puzzles although they were also used for scroll work and marquetry. The ability to produce sheets of thin wood was greatly improved, paving the way for plywood and thick card as new materials for jigsaw puzzles. This was a period of great advancement in the printing industry with the development of larger and more efficient presses and, in due course, colour printing.

Initially, however, maps continued to be the order of the day (see p98), to be followed (prior to 1800) by other educational subjects and, especially, historical tableaux. A popular theme was the kings and queens of England, each with a small portrait accompanied by some written details of the sovereign's reign (see p52). William Darton and John Wallis were two of the manufacturers who took over the dissected maps and pictures industry at this time and helped to propel it into the nineteenth century.

One early puzzle, dated about 1835, was an illustration of *The Ballad of John Gilpin*. In 1782 this witty and imaginative poem was published anonymously by its author, William Cowper, and three years later was included in public readings by an actor, John Henderson. It was an immediate success and within a very short time John Wallis, who was always quick to seize any new opportunity, manufactured puzzles of the ballad. It continued to be a popular jigsaw puzzle subject for many years but, more importantly, it established a whole new concept. Jigsaw puzzle subjects could be fun.

By 1800 the making of jigsaws was firmly established. In London, Darton and Wallis were established as the leading producers but others soon followed. The subject matter continued to be largely educational – maps, historical scenes, tables of sovereigns and, of course, the all-important biblical puzzles with illustrations from both Old and New Testaments. Nevertheless, the breakthrough had occurred and not only did jigsaw puzzles now have some lighter themes and a far wider range of educational subjects but, increasingly, catered for adults as well as children. The actual cutting of the puzzles would improve with more sophisticated jigsaws and the developing skill of the cutter.

In 1800 much of Europe was engulfed in war. The Battle of Trafalgar heralded England's victory over the French and the war gave great impetus to the industry of the country. The arrival of the steamship and the railway began a mighty leap forward in every section of national life.

During the nineteenth century, London continued to establish itself as the most important capital city in the world with business and commercial activities going hand-in-hand with its international prestige. It was in this atmosphere that jigsaw puzzle production expanded and developed. At the start of the century one of the major problems was the availability of the essential material for puzzles – wood. Obtaining the right sized sheets of mahogany or a similar wood was not easy because of the processes required to cut the wood into thin sheets. Only wood of high-quality would take such thin cutting and there was the possibility that the sheet would warp. A common feature of many older jigsaw puzzles, warping was sometimes so bad that the puzzle was, more or less, ruined. For this reason puzzles tended to be quite small and one manufacturer even offered a cheaper version of a puzzle with the sky omitted from the picture, because this reduced the amount of wood required. Only the more expensive boxes were made of oak or a similar hardwood and cheaper softwood or chip boxes were increasingly used.

From the outset the retail cost of jigsaw puzzles was a major concern. In 1815 a small jigsaw puzzle with thirty pieces could cost 5s (twenty-five pence) which was a considerable sum. However, at least labour was cheap and, as they were intended for children, most puzzles comprised only a few, large pieces. Moreover, while most puzzles had an interlocking border, the rest of the puzzle was simply and quickly cut with straight or wavy lines and a non-interlocking fit using a fairly primitive type of saw.

As the nineteenth century continued, the adult market for jigsaw puzzles steadily grew and puzzles became larger with many more and smaller pieces. Cutting became more intricate and, as a result, the production of a puzzle took far longer. Just a steady rise in the cutter's rate of pay meant a considerable increase in the price of puzzles, putting them beyond the reach of the great majority of the population. (By the beginning of the twentieth century a large puzzle could cost between £1 and £2 – for many, a week's wages.) Towards the end of the nineteenth century there were two helpful developments for the puzzle manufacturers. Firstly, the introduction of alternative materials, mainly plywood and cardboard. In England the makers tended to ignore the possibilities of cardboard which was in use in America, perhaps feeling it smacked of a 'cheap and cheerful' image. Good quality card of a reasonable thickness was certainly available and used for children's games such as *Misfits* where each figure was cut

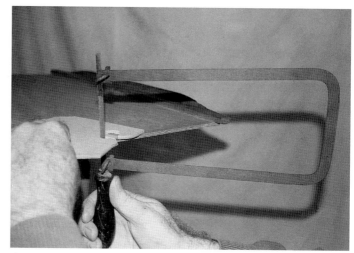

fig.1

fig.2. Dave Cooper on a treadle jigsaw.

into three parts horizontally and the pieces were interchangeable. However, the arrival of plywood provided the manufacturers with a cheaper and larger alternative for mounting their puzzles and the slightly softer nature of the wood, while it had its disadvantages in terms of durability, made cutting far easier and was helpful in prolonging the life of a saw-blade.

The second development involved the saw itself. A hand-held fretsaw has severe limitations in terms of accuracy; one hand holds the puzzle while the other has to guide and move the saw and it is easy when cutting the necks of the interlocking tags to make them too narrow so that they break (fig.1). The treadle-operated jigsaw proved to be the answer. With this type of saw (fig.2) the blade is powered with the foot and is static in a single vertical position. The cutter then has both hands free to move the puzzle and has greater control over the accuracy of the cut – it is both less tiring and quicker to cut a puzzle in this way. These improvements helped to combat rising labour costs during the century and to increase productivity. However, it remained a labour-intensive industry and larger puzzles continued to be expensive.

Competition is a vital stimulant in any creative and commercial enterprise and in this respect the jigsaw puzzle industry in London was fortunate. William Darton and his son set up in business in 1787 initially publishing books for children, but soon copied John Spilsbury's idea and began making educational dissections. Darton's puzzles were always of a high quality, if rather conservative in subject, and very much in line with the traditional Quaker beliefs of the Darton family that children should be educated and morally uplifted by their playthings. The Darton's firm flourished until the 1860s.

In 1775, John Wallis established a firm of booksellers and publishers and, with his sons John and Edward, the firm continued production until 1847. Wallis was a clever man, quick to see a good idea, especially from a rival, and to adapt and improve it. He saw the great potential of the children's market in books, games and puzzles and also recognised the need to make such items attractive and even lively, while other producers tended to remain stodgy and overly moralistic. His historical puzzle *Chronological Tables of English History for the Instruction of Youth* was a clear copy of Darton's puzzle published a year earlier but, simplified and more appealing, it deserved the great success it enjoyed. Wallis also combined games and jigsaw puzzles offering a double source of entertainment. He had an eye for publicity and marketing techniques, shown by his puzzle depicting the making of Royal Worcester china – a promotional ploy which was to become important in the developing story of the jigsaw puzzle.

Wallis' and his sons' business ethics were not inhibited by any Quaker scruples and they happily pirated ideas and material from their great rivals, the Darton firm. In fact, in 1813, Wallis printed a label for his puzzle-boxes claiming to be the inventor and first manufacturer of dissected puzzles, having made them for thirty years. This would put the date back to 1783 which is very doubtful and is, anyway, twenty-three years later than John Spilsbury's dissected map. However, by 1813, John Spilsbury was probably largely forgotten and but for Linda Hannas' research, Wallis might have got away with his false claim. John Wallis senior died in 1818 and the younger son, Edward, continued the family firm in London.

John Betts produced jigsaw puzzles from about 1830 to 1870 and was a dedicated educationalist (see p45). He advertised his games as 'invaluable as auxiliaries in the course of private education...and already in extensive use in the upper classes both in this country and in the colonies...'. Betts confined most of his activity to educational material, especially maps, but he also produced puzzles based on famous books such as *Robinson Crusoe* and *The Swiss Family Robinson*.

William Spooner, Nicholas Carpenter and James Izzard were puzzle manufacturers in the middle years of the nineteenth century and the firm of Arthur Park marketed the *Launch of The Thunderer, Fancy Fair* and *The Coronation of Queen Victoria*, rightly predicting the popularity of large ships and the royal family.

Linda Hannas has also done a remarkable piece of research to uncover the story of the Barfoots. These two leading producers of jigsaw puzzles showed a strange desire for anonymity as though, perhaps, they found their product a little beneath them – one of the Barfoots was a well-known miniaturist who exhibited his paintings in the Royal Academy. Particularly interesting is their price-list of jigsaw puzzles showing a range from 1s to 10s which was typical for this period (fig.3).

William Peacock and Raphael Tuck in particular were two companies who, in the last quarter of the century, paved the way for major developments in the jigsaw puzzle industry. Peacock was a major producer of jigsaw puzzles during the last twenty-five years of the nineteenth century. He specialised in double-sided geography/history puzzles and many are still to be found in their well-made boxes with *Peacock's Superior Dissection* proudly proclaimed on the labels. Some of the puzzles had a map on one side, usually published by Gall & Inglis, Philip & Son, or Crutchley, and a historical table on the other – kings and queens of England were the favourite. The puzzles,

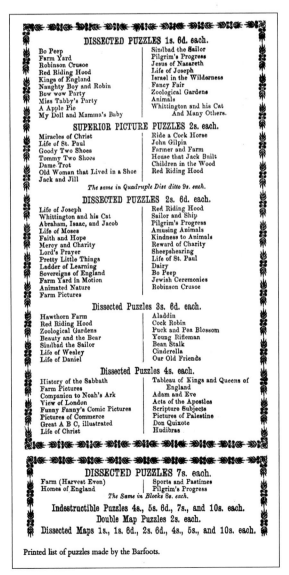

fig.3

mounted on hardwood and in wood boxes, were of exceptional quality for the period.

Cutting was usually to a set pattern with interlocking edges and then following the boundaries on the map in the middle. Despite their quality the puzzles were somewhat dull. No-one could doubt their educational intention but there was no effort to provide a challenge or ingenious variations. Perhaps the fact that so many have survived intact indicates that once a child had done the puzzle it was put away and rarely attempted again. Nevertheless, because of his prolific output, Peacock signalled the way for jigsaw puzzles in the twentieth century.

Raphael Tuck was altogether different. This German furniture dealer founded a firm of Fine Art publishers in London in 1870, and retired around 1882 leaving his three sons to continue the business. In about 1890 the firm began to make jigsaw puzzles and, by 1900, had a large output compared with their competitors, with premises in Paris and New York as well as London. The firm's main business was stationery and a list of 1902 details thirty different products but, strangely, does not include jigsaw puzzles. Nevertheless, the company made four very important contributions to jigsaw production as it entered the twentieth century.

Firstly, Tuck's felt no inhibitions or constraints about subject matter. They aimed to produce puzzles for all, and domestic scenes, children playing, scenes from Dickens, nursery rhymes and fairy stories, as well as the traditional maps, were all part of their developing range. Secondly, Raphael Tuck began a revolution in cutting by making the patterns far more intricate and introducing 'whimsies' (recognisable shapes like hatchets, legs, and bottles) into the puzzle (see p46). Thirdly, Tuck's pioneered the use of plywood and thick card in place of the expensive and easily warped hardwood sheets. The use of card also enabled Tuck's to experiment with a primitive form of die cutting which will be discussed later. Lastly, the company used attractively designed cardboard boxes for their puzzles with labels declaring that their puzzles were produced for 'Royalty, Society and the Great British Public', and small guide pictures were included on the side of the boxes.

During the period 1760 to 1900 there was a great increase in prosperity for a large part of the population. By 1900 many people were able to afford the time and money for recreational activities. Jigsaw puzzles were the ideal winter pastime, a perfect family entertainment on dark evenings. The hobby had come a very long way since its beginnings in 1760 and was poised for a period of extraordinary growth as the new century began.

CHAPTER 2
A RELEVANT SOCIAL HISTORY OF THE TWENTIETH CENTURY

The history of jigsaw puzzles during the twentieth century is closely tied to what was happening within society and the jigsaw puzzles themselves give us a wealth of information about social and other conditions. It is interesting, therefore, to review the century briefly and to note significant periods of change.

The beginning of the century saw the end of Queen Victoria's reign. For years some jigsaw puzzles had been anticipating the death of the Queen by depicting the kings and queens of England in their serried ranks and deliberately leaving an empty panel ready for Victoria. In the meantime, the puzzle manufacturer's name was discreetly placed in the panel pending the moment the aged monarch would oblige (fig.4).

fig.4

It was a time of great contrasts. The British Empire was dominant throughout the world, despite the recent war with the Boers in South Africa, and the areas coloured red on the many map puzzles of the time proclaimed Britain's worldwide dominion. Only the Queen herself, sombre and reclusive, still mourning her beloved Albert, cast a gloom over the nation. Yet even she had responded to the celebrations of her Diamond Jubilee three years before when there was a great outpouring of affection and national rejoicing. However, Britain was also a nation where poverty and industrial oppression kept the majority of the population deprived of either the money or the leisure time for jigsaw puzzles, books or games – an aspect of the sharp divide which existed within the Victorian society.

The accession of Edward VII brought some changes.

The contrast between son and mother was very marked, Edward lived a colourful, hedonistic life compared to the dour worthiness of Victoria's court, and the country looked to a brighter, more cheerful future. With the dawn of the Edwardian era many had happy expectations even though, in reality, there was little ground for such optimism.

The puzzles of the day reflected this change. The emphasis on education and morality remained, shown by the many puzzles on the subjects of history and geography and scenes from the Bible, and there were still the sentimental themes depicting children and animals. Now, however, more lively and robust puzzles began to emerge. The hunting theme was a good example of this – large numbers of puzzles were produced of bucolic huntsmen effortlessly clearing gigantic hedges as the hounds spread out in front, with the ladies of the hunt riding side-saddle and looking immaculate (see p61).

During this period there were many technological inventions to excite the jigsaw manufacturers. Ships and trains had long been a favourite subject – this was the era of the rapid development of the motor car and the invention of the aeroplane, and the puzzles of the time reflected the latest developments.

Meanwhile, as Edward's short reign progressed, there was an uneasy peace in Europe and storm clouds were on the horizon. British jigsaw puzzles did not show a great interest in the preparations for war – in contrast to other nations who used puzzles depicting battleships and the latest field guns as a means of blowing their national trumpets. National pride and confidence took a knock when the Titanic sank in 1912 and puzzles which had been contemplated of great unsinkable liners were probably quietly consigned to the waste-paper basket. Nevertheless, the main manufacturers like Tuck and Peacock continued to develop their ranges of puzzles, improving the quality and increasing production to meet a growing public demand (see pp62 and 63).

During the First World War, as part of their war effort, various combatant nations produced jigsaw puzzles both for propaganda purposes and for their troops' amusement. Whatever help or relief these may have offered the soldiers, jigsaw puzzles had a more important role at home. For the population this was a period of tension, waiting and fear. During the dark days of the war many a stressed family found a degree of peace sharing a puzzle, though jigsaw puzzles still remained the prerogative of the reasonably wealthy.

The years 1918 to 1939 were a most significant time for the jigsaw puzzle. A number of factors combined to create an unprecedented jigsaw craze. Despite the aftermath of war, unemployment, strikes, the stock market crash and the Depression, there was hope for a brighter future. It was a period of national optimism. This was an era of rapid and spectacular technical progress. World speed records were constantly being broken; distance records went the same way; worldwide communications improved; and the standard of living for the population as a whole rose, albeit very slowly.

At the same time, some degree of mass production was brought into jigsaw manufacture both for wooden and cardboard puzzles. When the Great Western Railway, a symbol of national pride and progress, published its range of jigsaw puzzles in 1924 they became very popular and sold out rapidly and, from then on, the G.W.R. added to the range until by 1939 a million puzzles had been sold (pp66-70).

This period saw new manufacturers using the latest methods of production. G.H. Hayter (who manufactured the Victory range of jigsaw puzzles) and Chad Valley were chief among these and the wide availability of their

"Seen my collar, Mildred?"
(1951)

Head of the Family (writing to the inventor, after wrestling with "The Best Puzzle of the Century"). "THE LEAFLET ACCOMPANYING YOUR UNHEALTHY INVENTION STATES THAT A PATENT HAS BEEN APPLIED FOR. YOU HAVE THE PRESENT STATE OF THE LAW TO THANK THAT A WARRANT HAS NOT ALSO BEEN APPLIED FOR."

fig.5 and 5a. *Punch* cartoons.

puzzles, even today, shows how successful they were in meeting public demand. Cutting improvements went hand-in-hand with far better pictures and an ever increasing range of subjects. Puzzles were the staple diet of many country house parties, as well as being found on ocean liners and express trains. Those who were unemployed, and who could afford jigsaw puzzles, used them to pass the time (figs.5 and 5a).

The jigsaw puzzle craze was infectious. It stimulated the manufacturers into increasing production and incorporating many new and original ideas. The national press responded by producing puzzles, and big stores like Woolworth sold their own line at 6d (2½ pence) each. With so much public interest other companies quickly followed the lead of the Great Western Railway and commissioned puzzles for advertising purposes – the Cunard White Star and Dunlop ranges of puzzles were among the best examples (see pp71-72, 84-85).

By 1939, however, economic factors were just beginning to have an effect. Then, the Second World War and the need for all materials, especially plywood, to be used in support of the war effort brought an end to almost all jigsaw puzzle production. Any puzzles that were produced were poor-quality, cardboard puzzles with inferior pictures often devoted to wartime subjects (see p88). It was considered lucky to get even those. My only wooden puzzle from this period is one my father cut for me using a hand-held fretsaw and I suspect it was the same for many others (see p73).

The war was followed, I suggest, by three periods in the twentieth century though it is difficult to be strictly precise.

1946-1960 – Christmas 1945 was a strange occasion with the nation trying to overcome the legacy of the war. Of course rationing continued but toys, games and jigsaw puzzle manufacturers made great efforts to re-stock the shops. As a result some very strange puzzles appeared which must have been pre-war stock. Many old prints were turned into puzzles and existing cut puzzles were tossed hurriedly into any available box. Thus, there is a puzzle depicting the landing of Johann Van Riebeeck at the Cape in 1652, in a blue later-series G.W.R. box, with correct guide picture and hand-written label on the spine (see p73).

It became apparent that the jigsaw puzzle industry could never be the same again. Production of wooden puzzles was extremely labour-intensive and labour costs had risen very significantly since 1939. The only solution, it seemed, was to supersede wooden puzzles with die-cut cardboard ones. In turn this decision created its own problems. How to achieve a sufficiently high-quality product to attract customers and, also, how to persuade them that cardboard puzzles were not inferior to the pre-war wooden ones? Both challenges proved difficult for the industry. Many of the puzzles of the period depict a brave, new, idyllic world but the reality was very different and the jigsaw craze of the pre-war years seemed to have evaporated (see p88). Meanwhile, the 1950s saw increased competition among various industries eager to influence the nation's use of leisure time.

1960-1975 – television had become a dominant force. The *Giles* cartoons at this time, often a good barometer of social trends, frequently depicted the whole family gathered around the television set in a near-hypnotic state (see p106). It was a period of rapid change, of new and exciting programmes and television made great strides in improving the scope and quality of its productions. A few jigsaw manufacturers tried to reap some benefit by featuring television personalities but the sales of puzzles and games, even such classics as *Monopoly*, declined during this period. However, though television undoubtedly reigned supreme there was still some limit to the amount of potted and passive entertainment that people would accept. The British have inventive and creative instincts and, in due course, many became bored with just watching the small screen.

Mid-1970s – the renaissance in hobbies began. There was a strong revival of interest in the past and people began to look back fondly to the days when 'we made our own entertainment' which was coupled with a growing movement to restore and preserve what was seen as valuable in our national heritage.

Assembling collections became popular during this time and jigsaw puzzles provided a perfect opportunity for collectors. Other aspects of jigsaw puzzles proved attractive. Many were in need of restoration, and this was the height of the 'Do It Yourself' period in the nation's history with enthusiasts ready and able to replace missing pieces and lovingly restore boxes.

Very few early production records survived and some collectors felt it important to undertake research so that comprehensive records could be built up and archives of material established. At the same time there was a great interest from museums, and special exhibitions were mounted. This period saw renewed interest in the British Jigsaw Puzzle Library and, in 1985, a worldwide jigsaw puzzle enthusiasts' club, the Benevolent Confraternity of Dissectologists, was founded. This developed alongside many similar clubs catering for people interested in a wide range of hobbies and activities.

In 1970, the opportunities for buying and selling among collectors were rather limited. *The Exchange and Mart* perhaps; a few small second-hand shops in the back streets of larger cities and towns; and, for the expensive and sought after item, a London auction room. Occasionally an advertisement in a local paper would unearth some treasure and it was always worth having a good look round a jumble sale. However, the period under review saw developments in the opportunities for collectors. There was an increase in collectors' magazines and papers, notably *The Collectors Gazette*, and also in the number of second-hand book-shops, and antique and bric-a-brac shops which began to specialise in smaller articles and 'ephemera' – a description which covered almost anything. The number of auction houses holding sales of smaller, lesser-value items for collectors also grew apace.

The major development, however, was the arrival of the swapmeet/toy fair and its offshoot, the car boot sale. By 1985, puzzles were an important element in many a swapmeet, fair and auction, and specialised jigsaw sections appeared in many auction catalogues. Several books had now been published about British and American jigsaw puzzles enabling the collector to be far better informed about his hobby.

In the 1990s there is an exciting range of new cardboard jigsaws being offered. The quality of these puzzles is excellent, the subjects are interesting and they are challenging to assemble. One aspect is of particular interest. In the 1920s and 1930s many puzzles depicted the latest developments in technology. For example, there were puzzles made using an artist's impression of the Queen Mary and issued before the ship had even been launched (see p75). The same can be said of the 1950s period with puzzles featuring the latest aircraft (see p103) and ships and, later, hovercraft. But in the 1990s puzzles of the Shuttle, space rockets or the latest cars are a rarity. The great majority of our new puzzles depict thatched cottages and villages of yesteryear, old cars, sailing ships, canal boats and, most popular of all it seems, scenes of the Great Western Railway in the glorious days of steam (see p121).

It seems that there is a widespread nostalgia for our grandparents' era and an interest in preserving our heritage, and the most popular subjects for our jigsaw puzzles reflect this.

CHAPTER 3

TECHNICAL DEVELOPMENTS IN THE TWENTIETH CENTURY

By 1900, interest in jigsaw puzzles was rapidly increasing. and there was a demand for larger and more challenging adults' puzzles. It should be emphasised that, because of its basic simplicity, the making of jigsaw puzzles is an unusual industry. Anyone can find a suitable picture, glue it to a thin piece of wood and, using a hand-held fretsaw, create a simple jigsaw puzzle and thousands of people did just that very skilfully (see Chapter 6). This posed problems for commercial manufacturers in a market which was highly labour-intensive and faced a great deal of competition from those who made jigsaw puzzles as a hobby. The industry had to develop and improve its technology and, fortunately, there was much scope for progress.

From the outset the material used dictated the whole technical process and its commercial implications. For the first eight decades of the century this was either wood or cardboard – I shall consider wood first, as it was the more important in the earlier years.

The demand was for larger puzzles with more pieces. To make the puzzle more challenging, smaller, intricately-cut pieces were required which had to fit cleanly and exactly. The hand-held fretsaw could not meet such a need. Its shape limited the size of puzzle that could be cut and its blades tended to be too coarse to cut a really intricate design or, if fine enough, then too easily broken. Moreover, as the saw had to be operated with one hand and moved up and down at speed, it was very difficult to keep the saw blade perfectly vertical. This resulted in a diagonal cut to the piece so it would only fit the next piece from one direction, and could be very frustrating when trying to assemble the puzzle (fig.6).

The treadle jigsaw, though in use by 1900, was at this stage in a rather primitive form and its development up to 1939 was in direct response to the needs of the industry. The larger tray and correspondingly long arm allowed a larger puzzle to be cut. Cutters of wooden puzzles always begin by reducing the whole puzzle to a number of pieces of manageable size – anything from 10cm to 25cm square

fig.7

is ideal – and do this by cutting the original puzzle in half, quarters or even eighths. The first cut is the challenge as a large piece of wood has to be manoeuvred on the tray and sometimes turned through nearly 360° to create a tab. If one looks carefully at a larger wooden puzzle it is possible to see where the cutter has made these original cuts in order to create easily managed pieces.

A treadle jigsaw allowed the cutter far more control. By powering the saw with his foot he was able to vary the speed of the blade. When cutting a straight line he could speed up, and when he came to an intricate turn, he could slow down. The saw (fig.7) was made as stable as possible with a heavy metal frame, usually of a tripod design, which was often quite ornate. A crank operated the main wheel drive from which the drive was taken to an upper flywheel by a belt. The earlier belts were leather, but rubber took its place often secured with a staple so that, as the belt stretched, a piece could be cut out and the staple easily replaced. From the upper flywheel a second crank took the drive to the head of the saw and here a variety of designs were tried.

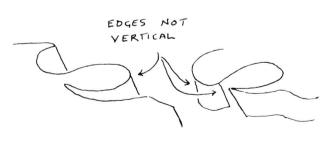

EDGES NOT VERTICAL

fig.6

16

Another requirement was a clean, vertical cut. This was the most challenging demand of all and dictated the whole design of the all-important head of the saw – the part where the blade was located and the means by which it was moved. The ideal was a fine blade which was tensioned so that it was straight, moved at varying speeds and was always perfectly vertical; also a blade with a long travel so that the maximum length of blade was used and it remained sharp for as long as possible (fig.8). This was difficult to achieve. Three types of head were tried (fig.9). These can be classified as upper arm moving; lower arm moving; both arms moving. The first two designs relied on a spring system to keep the blade tensioned [a]. The third involved a more rigid frame but was cumbersome and heavy in operation. Ultimately, the head of the saw was a compromise. If it was too heavy it would require excessive effort to move the blade at speed and get a clean cut; and there must be a certain amount of 'give' in the blade itself or, being fine, it would easily snap and much time would be lost replacing blades. The skill of the cutter was of great importance. The amount of pressure applied on the piece of wood would dictate how much the vertical blade would bend – and thus cease to be perfectly vertical. The cutter would have to perfect a combination of pressure and blade speed as well as using the most satisfactory angle for cutting, to ensure a clean, neat fit for the completed pieces. Cutting jigsaw puzzles was a very skilled task.

figs.10 and 10a. Chad Valley factory workers.

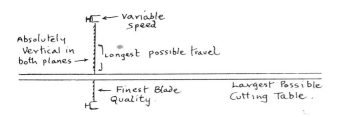

fig.8

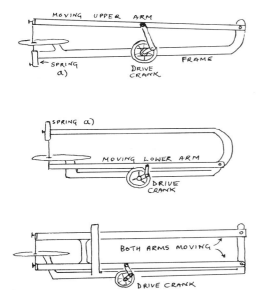

fig.9

During the first forty years of the century, the treadle jigsaw was modified but never radically so. A saw from 1900 is not very different to a 1940 model as demonstrated in the catalogues of Hobbies of Dereham, one of the largest saw manufacturers. Different cutters preferred one type of saw to another perhaps, but essentially it was a case of personal preference

Another factor was the need to lower costs. Cutting a wooden jigsaw was highly labour-intensive and expensive. To set up a whole line of cutters as in the Chad Valley factory was a case in point (figs.10 and 10a).

A solution was to cut more than one puzzle at a time. This was fairly easy when puzzles were the same picture and pinned together. The cutter then removed the pins as he cut the puzzle, making sure that his cut obliterated the hole made by the pin. This, however, created a problem. The strain on the blade was greatly increased and more likely to wander out of the vertical and, consequently, break more frequently. As a result, puzzle pieces that have been 'stack-cut' often fit less snugly.

There was another difficulty – I have a puzzle, *King George V* (the locomotive) by Chad Valley. The pieces fit perfectly but there is a line down the middle where the picture does not match up (see p73). The cutter stack-cut this puzzle and, having cut it in two, somehow muddled up the halves. So, somewhere, there is an identical mirror-image puzzle to mine!

The material used for the making of a jigsaw puzzle was fundamental. In 1900 there was a choice of two. One was thin slices of hardwood – mahogany and cedar were the favourites (old cigar boxes were made of similar thickness and type of wood) and, from about 1850, some soft woods were also used. The other and rarer material was 3mm cardboard which was cut with a large guillotine knife, sometimes designed to give a curved cut, but interlocking pieces and intricate designs were impossible. In the early years of the twentieth century the use of plywood became almost universal for wooden jigsaws. This had the advantages of being cheaper, easier to obtain, simpler to cut, and caused less wear and strain on delicate blades. The one disadvantage of plywood was that unless it was of the best quality, pieces tended to have a jagged and rough edge requiring much sanding. Occasionally, when poor quality plywood was used, pieces would actually break up where the original slices of wood in the sheet had not been properly glued together. To counter this, however, there were two advantages to plywood. It was rather less likely to warp over the years than the thin hardwood and, also, huge puzzles now became a possibility if sheets of plywood measured 8ft by 4ft.

A second important development was the availability of more and improved pictures for puzzles. During this century we have progressed from the hand-printed lithograph, coloured pretty crudely at times by children using stencils, to the most sophisticated colour prints. The range of pictures available to manufacturers at the end of the twentieth century and the quality of reproduction, means that the variety and quality of jigsaw puzzles is breathtaking compared to a century ago. Adhesives for fixing the picture to the base material are also excellent so that problems of pictures lifting off the pieces are very rare with modern puzzles.

As has been noted, the Second World War had a devastating effect on the jigsaw puzzle industry. Plywood and other woods were needed for the production of war materials – the Mosquito aircraft was partly built of plywood! The men who had cut the puzzles were called up – Chad Valley had employed fifty at its peak – and the women moved into the munitions factories.

However, because of the war, there was a great improvement in the types and uses of metals which helped with the production of cutting dies for cardboard jigsaw puzzles. Cutting a cardboard or thin wooden jigsaw with a die, dated from the later nineteenth century when thin steel blades were set in a wooden block in such a way that a small non-interlocking puzzle could be stamped out. By the 1920s a thinner grade of cardboard was used which made the stamping process easier, hence the blades of the die could be thinner. In turn, this meant they were more easily bent and so a fully interlocking puzzle could be stamped out. Quality remained a problem and cardboard puzzles from the twenties and thirties often have pieces which are not properly separated due to damaged or worn blades in the die, or a faulty press. I remember, as a boy, spending many hours with a modelling knife cutting up a cardboard puzzle that was totally stuck together. Another

fig.11. Howard and John, form makers at Waddington's.

problem was that the press was not large enough to deal with a sizeable picture. I have a puzzle from the late 1940s which has been pressed out into two halves which then have to be laid side-by-side to form the completed picture (see p92).

After the war it became clear that commercially the future lay with the cardboard puzzle, and the 1950s saw great improvements in range and quality. Waddington's and Tower Press led the way, with many other makers hard on their heels. Three factors contributed to this improvement: pictures for puzzles continually improved and there was a wealth of subjects including new technological developments and nostalgic scenes; the quality of cardboard improved, becoming thicker and denser in composition so that a cleaner cut was obtained and pieces were harder wearing; and the presses had an increased capacity and were more efficient allowing ever-larger puzzles to be produced more quickly and to a very high standard.

By the 1990s, Waddington's at Leeds was one of the few manufacturers who undertook the complete production of cardboard puzzles from start to finish. Once

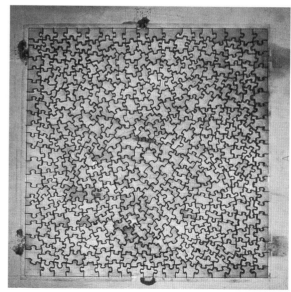

fig.12

the size and number of pieces of a puzzle are determined, the form-maker goes to work on it (fig.11). On a sheet of 15mm plywood he marks out the size of the puzzle with each piece as a small square. He uses a 9mm steel band and using a variety of dies, bends this to shape on a hand-press. Long bands, shaped, are set into the plywood board parallel to one another right across the board. The gaps between are then filled with smaller shaped bands to make the shape for each individual piece of the puzzle. (It takes four-and-a-half weeks to make the complete form for a 500-piece circular puzzle.) The bands, which have a razor-sharp top edge, are held in place with small pins so that the finished form resembles a large and extremely intricate pastry cutter (fig.12). A rubber mat about 8mm thick is then pressed down on to the cutters and each space is filled with rubber which projects beyond the blade of the cutter. The form is then fitted into the top of the press which pushes it down with great force.

The largest press is the Sheridan. The Samco, a smaller version, is widely used while the older Oyster presses have been replaced by their modern equivalents built by Hawks Technical and Bobst (fig.13). The press has to be very powerful because of the large length of blade that is pressed cleanly through the board. Also the lower bed of the press upon which the puzzle will rest, has to be very carefully prepared to ensure a perfectly clean cut for the puzzle. If it is not, the pieces will be attached to one another and damage will ensue. Meanwhile, the pictures and the board are glued together in a large machine and when dry are trimmed by a guillotine.

fig.13

The Sheridan press is double-sided and its two operators have to work in synchronisation. The puzzle is placed on the bed, pressed, and then lifted out with the next puzzle slid underneath it, and placed, still fully assembled, on a conveyor belt. It is checked before going into a machine that breaks up the puzzle and bags the pieces. Each bag is labelled with the code number of the puzzle and it then passes to the part of the plant where it is boxed and packed. The main elements in this process for manufacturing cardboard puzzles have not changed significantly during the second half of the century – some

of the presses in use at Waddington's in the 1990s were nearly thirty years old.

While commercial pressures may have forced manufacturers to favour cardboard, the day of the wooden jigsaw puzzle was by no means over. After the war the electric jigsaw (fig.14) was developed and became the obvious tool for the amateur cutter and those producing specialist and commissioned jigsaw puzzles although some craftsmen continued to prefer their treadle jigsaw because of the greater control of blade speed .

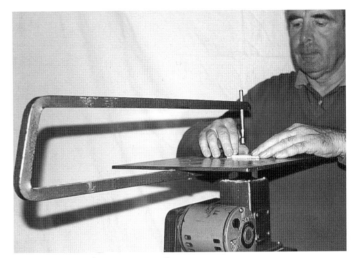

fig.14. The author using an electric jigsaw.

Basically, the electric jigsaw comes in two varieties. The early type consisted of a table and arm with a saw head very similar to a treadle jigsaw, the blade usually being tensioned by a spring above, and held by a moving clamp below the tray. The moving bit is connected to a crank which is driven in turn by a geared down electric motor. The whole saw, while of necessity quite heavy, sits easily on a workbench or table, and is mains-operated (fig.15). It is possible to exchange the spring-loaded top fixing for the blade with a simple tube in which the end of the blade slides freely. This means that the blade is far less likely to break, but making a perfectly vertical cut demands greater skill from the cutter. A number of different methods of sawdust extraction have also been tried so that the cutter does not have to stop working in order to blow sawdust away.

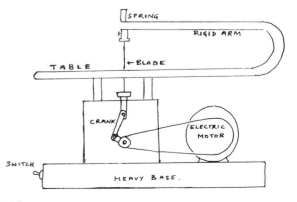

fig.15

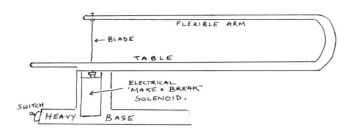

fig.16

Later in the century a new type of jigsaw was developed using a solenoid with a make-and-break electrical contact instead of a motor. This machine (fig.16) is less cumbersome than the other, though it can suffer from its lack of weight and consequent instability. It has two other problems. Firstly, the blade speed, which cannot be varied, is extremely fast and therefore it is easier to make cutting errors. Secondly, the blade travel is small which means that only a small part of the blade is used and it becomes more easily blunted. However, these saws are moderately priced and suitable for the amateur who wishes to cut an occasional puzzle.

Commercial manufacturers of wooden jigsaw puzzles had to use a saw which would enable them to stack-cut up to eight puzzles at a time. This required a much thicker blade and a more powerful saw to drive it (fig.17). Operators would stand in order to better manipulate the puzzle being cut, and work with incredible speed so that up to 1600 wooden pieces could be cut in an hour. While this made the operation commercially viable it also resulted in a rather loose fit for the pieces. Most puzzles being produced by these manufacturers were for the children's market.

One other important development in wooden puzzles should be mentioned – making replacements of damaged or missing pieces. As older wooden puzzles have increased in value it has become worthwhile to have replacement pieces made, though the presence of the replacement is always notified and will obviously detract from the value

fig.17

fig.18. Val Cooper painting replacement pieces for jigsaw puzzles.

of the puzzle. The process usually involves at least seven stages. The pieces surrounding the missing piece have to be assembled so that the gap is exactly accurate. Suitable paper or card can then be slid under the pieces, and a tracing made with a very sharp pencil. This is then stuck on to a piece of wood of the correct thickness and texture to match the puzzle as nearly as possible and, when dry, it is cut out using a jigsaw. The blank white piece is fitted and, as a rule, has to be sanded and filed to ensure a perfect fit. It is then put into place and painted with acrylic or oil paint which is, perhaps, the most skilled part of all. Finally the new piece can be glazed or varnished to match the sheen of the original puzzle as closely as possible (fig.18).

In the later 1990s Alison Norton, a graduate of Newcastle University, did a research project on the conservation of objects made of wood and paper and, in particular, jigsaw puzzles. She investigated the effect of acidity, dampness, changes in temperature and other factors in causing the pieces of a wooden jigsaw to deteriorate. Of perhaps equal interest, when restoring an old puzzle Alison has used a laser to scan the relevant part from a guide picture, and then glued this to a wooden replacement piece. This is a particularly accurate way of matching colours and pictures when making a replacement piece for one of the late eighteenth- or early nineteenth-century puzzles. It can also be used when some of the required colour is still available on the puzzle with missing pieces – for example, when replacing sky pieces which are often among the most difficult to colour match.

It is relevant at this point to draw attention to jigsaw puzzle boxes and packing. In 1900 both wooden and cardboard boxes were used. For economy, wood boxes were usually made of softwood and had sliding lids with a guide picture on them (see p51). Cardboard boxes were made of stiff cardboard with either a lift-off lid or, as with Tuck's puzzles, a hinged lid that opened back on to a supporting strut. The plastic bag was yet to be invented and the main concern of the manufacturer was to make a box of such design and quality that small puzzle pieces would be well protected.

After the First World War virtually all boxes were of cardboard and a number of different designs were tried. These can best be illustrated by the series of boxes by Chad Valley for their promotional puzzles. It began with a simple box with a base tray and lift-off lid. Staples were used in its construction but the card was not robust and the staples rusted. The seams tended to come apart so jigsaw pieces were easily lost. In the early 1930s a sleeve box was designed to stack on a shelf like a book. This had two disadvantages. Friction when sliding the box open and shut weakened the two parts of the box and, when pulled open with speed, pieces were easily scattered. Chad Valley then designed a book box with two trays which opened like a book and which was secured with a tape to keep it shut. In my view this was the best box ever produced – strong, secure and visually attractive but it was expensive and, after the Second World War, Chad Valley reverted to the original tray box with lift-off lid, though now better made and without the staples. Chad Valley and other makers sealed their boxes before they left the factory and prospective purchasers were instructed to make sure the seals were intact. There was also a checker's label inside the box. Incidentally, should a piece go missing, some manufacturers, such as Chad Valley, offered their own piece-replacement service.

The hazards of poor-quality boxes of this period can be seen in a box in my possession which opens at one side and both ends and seems designed to scatter its small cardboard pieces. In contrast, I also have a rare cardboard puzzle from this period, depicting two swallows, which is not only in a sturdy cardboard box but is also enclosed in a cloth bag tied with tapes. As a result, it is still complete. Poor-quality boxes continued to be a feature of the puzzle industry during the 1950s.

Manufacturers such as Waddington's led the way in improving boxes, and design was almost always the lift-off lid type. The arrival of the plastic bag created a revolution allowing the puzzle to be sealed in and eliminating the danger of losses from a leaky box. Boxes in the 1990s are of a high quality and also extremely attractive, usually with a guide picture occupying much of the box lid in contrast to the small or even non-existent guide pictures in the earlier part of the century.

Mention should also be made of the extremes of size in puzzles. The smallest I have seen is a puzzle measuring about 10cm square with about 120 pieces, cut using a water-jet technique. To assemble this, one really needs a pair of tweezers and a magnifying glass (see p101). The largest puzzle I have done – with friends – measured 10ft

fig.19

by 40ft. This featured one of the posters used by the Ford Motor Co. (fig.19) and is interesting for the following reasons. It must be unique that a puzzle required about ten sheets of plywood to back it; it was cut out using a hand-held jigsaw of the type used by carpenters rather than jigsaw cutters; and the pieces are fully interlocking and about 2ft square!

In the last decade of the twentieth century two new methods of cutting puzzles have been tried in an effort to produce wooden jigsaw puzzles that are commercially competitive. One method is using water-jets and the other, laser beams. The water-jet uses a very fine, high-pressure jet of water to cut the pieces of the puzzle. This is not a new idea – it has long been known that a high-pressure water-jet has a remarkable power of penetration and such jets have been used in different industrial processes for many years. In this case the water is passed through a diamond jet at a force of 40-50,000 lbs per square inch, and emerges from the jet at twice the speed of sound. Every type of material from card to armoured steel, of thicknesses up to $1\frac{1}{2}$ ins, can be cut, though when metal is cut an abrasive is added to the water. The material to be cut is held in position over a large tank of water which absorbs the force of the jet after cutting and the jet moves around above it, controlled by a computer. One machine has six jets which cut simultaneously. Gee Graphite Ltd., founded by Colin Gee of Mirfield, Yorkshire (fig.20), is one of the pioneers of this method of industrial cutting and Colin and his wife, Pauline, have

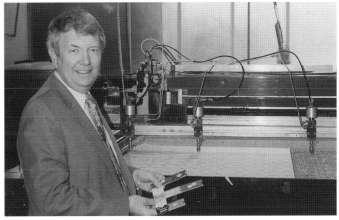

fig.20. Colin Gee.

done much experimentation in the whole field of water-jet cutting. As a result they have set up a separate company, Jigsaw Dimensions, to produce wooden jigsaw puzzles. They are using their computer to make interchangeable jigsaw pieces, about which, more later. Colin Gee is not only able to produce minute wooden jigsaw puzzles (5$\frac{1}{2}$cm x 7$\frac{1}{2}$cm with 165 pieces) but he also produces tablemat jigsaw puzzles made from carpet tiles. In fact he is able to use almost any material to make a jigsaw puzzle.

By 1980 Robert Longstaff of Longworth, near Abingdon, was producing miniatures, toys and puzzles and experiencing all the problems associated with a labour-intensive industry. As a physicist, he decided to experiment with a laser for cutting puzzles and though his first efforts were unsuccessful, a chance meeting with an eye surgeon convinced Robert that, given the right laser, cutting should be possible and by 1986 he had succeeded.

Thanks to the new technology a revolution was about to take place. The wooden jigsaw puzzle had been eclipsed by the cardboard puzzle because of high production costs. However, there now existed a machine which could automatically cut a puzzle.

In both the laser cutting and water-jet cutting processes the wooden puzzle is positioned over a specially designed tray beneath the laser head or water-jet. There are then two alternatives. Either the cutting head can move, or else the tray, and there are a number a of different methods to achieve the detailed and precise movement necessary. The great advantage of these cutting techniques is the speed that can be achieved in the cutting of wooden puzzles up to 1200 pieces. The speed of cutting now makes the wooden jigsaw puzzle conomically viable. With both the water-jet and laser cutting techniques the computer technology is as essential and impressive as the cutting mechanism itself. The proposed design of cut is fed into the computer – a very skilled and challenging process – which then dictates the necessary directions to move either the cutting head or tray, and cut the design on to the puzzle. Without this computer technology the process would be impossible and it is the computer which gives great flexibility to the process and means different cutting designs can be stored and re-used.

All modern producers of wooden jigsaw puzzles, whether using traditional cutting methods or water-jets and lasers, are able to take advantage of new materials like M.D.F. board and a greater variety of plywoods, as well as new and very effective adhesives for sticking the picture to the board. The quality achieved today is exceptionally good thanks to all these technical advances.

Quite remarkably, a trend which started with the arrival of the cardboard jigsaw puzzle at the beginning of the century looks as though it could be reversed in these last years of the 1990s.

Steve Richardson, the founder of Stave Jigsaw Puzzles in Norwich, Vermont, U.S.A. produces jigsaw puzzles which are among the finest in the world. They are cut with traditional power jigsaws using mahogany backed 5-plywood. In 1989 Steve was desperately trying to find a new way of hoodwinking and frustrating his fanatical customers and he stumbled on a secret that has eluded jigsaw puzzle cutters since 1760. This is the interchangeable piece – the piece which will fit perfectly in two or more places in the puzzle but only one place is correct. In a puzzle containing dozens of such pieces the permutations are enormous, as is the frustration! However, as already indicated, the versatile computer is already able to perform the same feat.

The construction of three-dimensional jigsaw puzzles was pioneered in America and Canada with unsatisfactory results at times, primarily because of the poor quality of the pieces. In 1996 Waddington's began production and an immediate problem was the bulkiness of the materials. The foam backing for the puzzles is about 7mm thick, compared with the 4mm plywood. Therefore, the 718-piece *Washington Capitol Building* puzzle has to be accommodated in a box measuring 10cm x 30cm x 40cm. One of the most important parts of the process is glueing the paper to the foam backing and drying the material, and though Waddington's achieved this to a higher standard than other manufacturers, breaking up the pieces for packing can be something of a problem, and the puzzle sometimes arrives with as many as seven pieces joined together.

On the *Capitol Building* the top dome is supported by a framework of thick cardboard and the dome itself is made of thin card which is pressed out and assembled using slots and tabs (see p112). This aspect of the puzzle is clearly a modelling operation and has little to do with jigsaw puzzles. In fact the whole concept is a hybrid of the two, though no less interesting and challenging for that and the range of 3-D puzzles is exciting with even the *Millennium Falcon* featured (see p112).

During this century, there have been extraordinary technical developments in every aspect of of jigsaw puzzle production. Due to the recent developments the wooden jigsaw puzzle now has an exciting future. The industry will, however, have to find presses to replace the ageing Sheridan and Samco models for pressing the larger cardboard puzzles. Yet, in Yorkshire, Peter Stocken and his family are still producing jigsaw puzzles of superb quality using treadle jigsaws and methods which would have been almost identical to those of 1900. It is this rich variety and contrast which augurs well for the jigsaw puzzle industry in the new millennium.

CHAPTER 4

COMMERCIAL PRESSURES AND INFLUENCE, RARITY AND PRICES

A significant factor in the commercial production of wooden puzzles is the ability of individuals to produce, as a hobby, puzzles of equal quality. Consequently, jigsaw puzzle production has always had to be commercially viable in a tightly competitive market. In the early part of the century, cutting was done by the treadle jigsaw and was highly labour-intensive. Puzzles were stack-cut by a cutter concentrating on the same puzzle each time and production was fast. Even so it was costly despite cheap labour in the period before the First World War. In the period 1918 to 1939 the effects of the Depression made the marketing of jigsaw puzzles, which were regarded as luxury items, difficult. Many unemployed people bought a small saw and started making and selling jigsaw puzzles thus providing tough competition for the manufacturers.

In 1924 Chad Valley produced the first jigsaw puzzles for the Great Western Railway and when these failed to sell at the retail price of 5s for a 150-piece puzzle, they were sold for 2s6d, the cost price. Later puzzles had about 200 pieces and were stack-cut. Chad Valley managed to keep production costs the same into the 1930s but, in 1937, reduced the number of pieces to 150 again, to curb rising costs. It was the cutting time for a puzzle which dictated cost and competitiveness.

After 1945 the commercial battle was between the cardboard and the wooden puzzle. Initially, people were willing to pay far more for a wooden puzzle than for an 'inferior' cardboard one. However, this changed as the quality of cardboard puzzles improved while wooden ones remained expensive, had fewer pieces and were designed for children.

Demand for jigsaw puzzles slackened in the 1950s and some companies went out of business. The 1970s saw the start of two very important trends in the jigsaw puzzle industry: a resurgence of interest, coupled with a demand for larger and more difficult puzzles; and the realisation that older jigsaw puzzles, especially the wooden ones, had become collectable items.

The increasing demand for jigsaw puzzles in the last three decades of the twentieth century has created new companies and encouraged existing ones to expand their range. In addition, advanced technology has enabled wooden jigsaw puzzle production to be commercially viable once again, and cardboard puzzles have become larger and of better quality. There have been the inevitable mergers and takeovers among the companies but the industry is in good heart and has a brighter future than for many years.

Towards the millennium there is a wider diversity than ever and much of this is due to commercial pressures. Sara White, a traditional cutter of wooden puzzles, ranks as one of the most skilled and imaginative in the country. She charges £6 per hundred pieces for her superb puzzles and has a very full order book. Optimago, in London, market a most attractive copy of William Powell Frith's *Railway Station* with 600 pieces for £37.45.

Commercial pressure has led companies to experiment with laser-cutting which can be computer-programmed and is the nearest one can get to an automated production line in wooden puzzles – and cutting with water-jets has been tried for the same reason (see Chapter 3). The advent of cutting by laser and the ability to cut a 250-piece wooden jigsaw in a very short time, has radically changed the situation. There is no doubt that for many reasons most people prefer wooden puzzles and to be able to buy both adults' and children's puzzles at a fraction of their former cost will create a larger market and transform the industry. There is also every likelihood that, as with other technology, the machines now in use will become smaller and cheaper.

During the last two decades of the twentieth century there has been a great increase in interest in second-hand puzzles. This book is not a price guide to old and rare puzzles but it will give some general indications of value.

The concept of 'collectable' items – those that command a high price because of age, rarity and appeal – is a peculiarly twentieth-century one. Many of our Victorian ancestors tended to throw away or demolish anything that was old, believing that they could make or build better than preceding generations, and the consequences of such attitudes are with us to this day. Collecting antique furniture was becoming popular by the 1920s but really came into its own after the Second World War, with the important American influence affecting the market. In the same period items such as stamps, medals and coins became collectable and, by the 1970s, so did a rapidly growing group of subjects including tinplate and die-cast toys, dolls, pipes, china and glassware, games and playing cards, cigarette cards, old annuals, and rare books. During the 1970s jigsaw puzzles began to be sought after. A few wise and dedicated enthusiasts had already begun their collections, rescuing many older puzzles from destruction. In particular, we owe Linda Hannas our gratitude for collecting and preserving so many irreplaceable eighteenth- and nineteenth-century puzzles.

The early jigsaw puzzle industry, as most other toy and

games industries, kept very poor production records, so early collectors had little idea of the range of puzzles made, or their relative rarity. During the later 1970s some friends and I kept a record of all the G.W.R. puzzles which appeared as a sort of 'league table'. After a couple of years it was clear that some of the puzzles were much rarer than others because far fewer had been produced – either because the subject proved unattractive, or the run had been cut short by the war.

In the mid-1970s most G.W.R. puzzles sold for between £5 and £10 depending on subject and condition – the railway scenes having the edge. Within about fifteen years the most common G.W.R. puzzles fetched about £20 - £25 and the rarest could reach £400 at auction. One puzzle, *Lost in Transit*, which was made of thick card and issued to the G.W.R. goods staff to encourage gentle handling of parcels, is very rare as most were probably consigned to the dustbin on receipt! *Lost in Transit* has fetched successively over £600 and £900 at auction in the 1990s, two of the highest prices ever reported for a puzzle (see p111). There are certain broad guidelines when collecting jigsaw puzzles:

1. Older puzzles are more valuable than newer ones. Produced in smaller numbers, they have an historical interest.

2. Puzzles identified with a maker's name and address and a date, are more valuable than anonymous ones.

3. Wooden puzzles are more valuable than cardboard ones.

4. Advertising puzzles and promotional puzzles are sought after and command higher prices.

5. Certain subjects have more appeal: royalty, transport, natural history, birds and animals, historical and military scenes, cartoon characters, and well-known personalities.

6. Certain subjects have less appeal: rural cottage scenes, harbour scenes, alpine villages, groves of trees, even when in autumn foliage!

The only sensible criteria for collecting, however, is that a particular puzzle, or range of puzzles, appeals to you. To allow for proper inspection, jigsaw puzzles must be assembled before purchase. Pieces can be replaced (see Chapter 3) but this is expensive and, however good, will reduce the value of any puzzle. Thus there is a point when it is not worth replacing pieces – say more than three – unless the puzzle is very rare or there are sentimental reasons for wanting it complete.

What governs the actual value of a puzzle? If a puzzle is very attractive or interesting but millions of copies are in circulation, it will not be valuable. If it is very rare, but the subject is unappealing, again it will not be valuable. It is the combination of rarity and appeal which dictates its value. When a contemporary image by a popular artist is used, such as Mabel Lucie Attwell (see p80), then the puzzle also appeals to another maket and its value is greatly enhanced. The most collectable of the standard Chad Valley G.W.R. puzzles is an interesting picture of the locomotive assembly shop at Swindon (see p69). This

apparently had a very short production run and is, consequently, scarce. As a result an excellent example made about £400 at auction in the mid-1990s. The much commoner mid-range G.W.R. puzzles are around £60.

The next factor is its condition. The puzzle may be in a generally poor condition. A few puzzles were so badly cut that some pieces were damaged before the puzzle even left the factory. The paper may have lifted off the pieces, or been torn. Tabs or thin protrusions may have broken off and poor quality plywood may have disintegrated. The condition of the box, or the absence of one, makes a significant difference to value. If there is no box I would reduce the value by at least 30%, and probably 50% if a rare collector's item. If the box is crushed, torn or damaged, a 20% - 40% reduction should be made. If it is badly worn, or the guide picture torn, make a 10% - 15% reduction. If the puzzle and box are in good condition but missing one piece, I would deduct 15% - 25% depending on the position of the gap and its effect on the puzzle. For subsequent missing pieces, up to a total of six, 5% each. If more than six pieces are missing, it is doubtful whether restoration is worthwhile, and I would reduce the value to 10% - 20%. If more than a dozen pieces are missing you are just paying for the box! If pieces are broken, or tabs missing, I would halve the above depreciation figures. Ultimately, however, each buyer has to judge the overall condition of a puzzle, and estimate its worth to him or her. When I began to build my collection of G.W.R. puzzles, I took any puzzles that filled a gap (including one *Freight Train* with seventeen pieces missing), in the hope that I could eventually upgrade my collection. This indeed happened and most of my collection is now complete and good.

Looking at the jigsaw puzzle market in the later 1990s there is a wide range of prices even when puzzles are in good condition, complete and boxed. The cheapest are cardboard puzzles made in the last quarter of this century and of less attractive subjects. These were produced in large quantities and are readily available second-hand in charity shops and at car boot sales. They are priced between 50 pence and £5 depending on size and subject.

Cardboard puzzles from the 1945 to 1975 period are rarer. Ranges like the Tower Press *Good Companion Series* and Waddington's *Circular Puzzles* are attractive and most collectable. These will vary in price from £4 to £15. Pre-war cardboard puzzles are rare and unlikely to be in good condition. They cost from £12 - £25 plus, and most will be in the hands of collectors.

Adults''s wooden puzzles in the last quarter of this century were made by a limited number of manufacturers and usually in small numbers compared with cardboard. Subjects have been carefully chosen, and thus they will hold their value fairly well. They will be in the £20 - £40 price range.

During the years 1918 to 1939 a number of firms such as Tuck, Chad Valley, Salmon and Victory were in full production but not many of these puzzles have survived. There are also many large and beautifully cut puzzles by little-known manufacturers, and even individual cutters, from this period. If the few extremely rare and sought-after puzzles already mentioned are discounted, there is still a very wide price range. Relatively common puzzles of rural scenes, seaside views, garden and cottage pictures by Chad Valley and Victory will be in the £13 - £25 price band. Rarer ones by Tuck, Salmon, A.V.N. Jones and others will be £20 - £40 range. During this period there were many puzzles of the Royal Family and these are always popular and, depending on size and subject, are in the region of £30 - £45 (see p54). There were also many transport subjects and, in particular, the promotional puzzles made by Chad Valley for Cunard/White Star, British India, Dunlop and the G.W.R. These puzzles are mainly within the £40 - £150 price range, with the rarer G.W.R. puzzles fetching over £300. The Victory and Jones transport subjects from this period fetch less – usually £30 - £70. This was the period when production of the wooden jigsaw puzzle was at its height, and many good examples have survived. There were high-quality puzzles of exciting subjects but there were also many poor-quality puzzles with commonplace subjects hence the wide range in values.

In the period 1945 to 1975 well-known companies such as Chad Valley and Victory went out of business. Though their puzzles are fairly common they are, nevertheless, found at auctions and in a few specialised shops and collectors will advertise them. Prices range from £25 - £70, again depending on subject and size – Victory *Gold Box* puzzles for example, average £30 - £45. There are some rare puzzles which were produced briefly just after the war and these are very collectable.

Puzzles from 1900 to 1918 are not so prolific mainly because Chad Valley and Victory were not yet in existence. Companies like Holtzapffel and Tuck produced a range of excellent, if rather expensive, puzzles with an attractive choice of subjects. In good boxed condition these puzzles tend to be rare and also because of their age are sought after by collectors. Prices will be in the £50 - £200 range.

Finally, children's puzzles. These are puzzles with less than 100 and often less than 50 pieces. Subjects vary from transport and rural scenes to nursery rhymes and animals. Victory, in particular, produced an excellent range of wooden puzzles for children some, such as the *Jungle Scene* and *Farm Scene*, over a very long period. As a general rule, one should expect to pay half the price of an adults' puzzle for a children's one, whether wood or cardboard (see pp80, 94 and 102).

From 1960 to date, a very wide range of both wooden and cardboard children's puzzles have been produced by a variety of manufacturers including Waddington's, Spears and Falcon. These have often been linked to film and television characters and a large number of Walt Disney creations. They are readily available second-hand and cost from 50 pence to £2. Condition is a key factor when valuing children's puzzles.

I would emphasise that this chapter should only be taken as a rough guide to jigsaw puzzle prices. A puzzle is worth what someone will pay for it as an addition to his or her collection.

CHAPTER 5

HISTORIES OF REPRESENTATIVE TWENTIETH-CENTURY JIGSAW PUZZLE MANUFACTURERS

The manufacturers discussed in this chapter have been chosen for one of three reasons. Firstly, because they have a long history of production and their puzzles are widespread and significant to the jigsaw puzzle scene. Secondly, because their puzzles are so distinctive in subject matter and quality, they are highly collectable and have become milestones in the history of the century's puzzles. Thirdly, because of technical innovation or some other feature of production, the company is a trend-setter in the industry.

Raphael Tuck

Raphael Tuck came to England in 1866, aged forty-four, and founded a business in London initially selling pictures and frames. He soon added publishing and the production of prints including, in 1871, the first commercially produced Christmas cards. In 1893 Tuck received the Royal Warrant from Queen Victoria for printing the Queen's letter to the nation on the occasion of the death of the Duke of Clarence.

In 1894 Tuck's produced the first picture postcard and, soon after, began selling children's jigsaw puzzles (cut with dies – steel cutting bands locked between blocks of wood) with a domestic or religious theme. By the end of the century, jigsaw puzzles had become a well-established part of the company's increasingly diverse range. Yet, though the firm's letterheads in 1902 and 1904 list thirty products, there is no mention of jigsaw puzzles.

Raphael Tuck died in 1900, and his two sons took over the company which included Sir Arthur Conan Doyle as one of its directors, and in 1909 launched their famous *Zag-Zaw* puzzles. The inscription on the distinctive red boxes for the puzzles makes impressive reading:

'Incomparably the Best. The Original British Made Tuck's Zag Zaw \ The Royal Picture Puzzle. A most fascinating recreation, used by Royalty, Society and the great public.'

The puzzles were extremely well cut, with a profusion of whimsies, including axes, bones, hats, airships, figures, shoes, birds etc. Boxes were of a high quality and sealed to protect the contents. By 1914 Raphael Tuck was a leading producer of jigsaw puzzles in the United Kingdom with a flourishing export market, especially to America. Moreover, with the introduction of specifically adults' puzzles of excellent quality, Tuck's can be credited with initiating the puzzle craze which was to sweep across the Atlantic. Before the outbreak of war, Tuck's had produced a superb 1250-piece wooden puzzle entitled *The House of Lords*. Further, the company recognised the advantages of using the new plywood for jigsaw puzzles and soon used this in its wooden puzzle production.

In the early 1920s, Tuck's combined their two most popular products and created the 'puzzle postcard' made from a postcard to be sent through the post. These were a great success and soon the company was marketing them in packets of six. These arrived with instructions for use in party games – a form of race with score sheets included. 'Picture puzzle playing has caught on, and is becoming a formidable rival of Bridge' announced the English weekly magazine, *Truth*. Many other companies rushed to follow in Tuck's footsteps, both in Europe and America.

A Raphael Tuck catalogue from the mid-1920s lists and illustrates about two hundred and forty different puzzles ranging from 55 to 1000 pieces. The subjects chosen were interesting, especially in comparison to the puzzles being produced by Victory and Chad Valley. Early-century liners were greatly outnumbered by sailing ships and the only warships were Nelson's *Victory* (see p96) and those of similar vintage. Other subjects were landscape, seascape, romantic, pastoral, hunting and children. Many pictures were by well-known artists including J.M.W. Turner, Holman Hunt, E.J. Andrews, J. Spurling and George Studdy, creator of *Bonzo* (see p80). There is not a car, railway train or aeroplane in sight even though this is the mid-1920s. The catalogue has the ambience of the last days of the nineteenth century – the clock turned back as though the awful events of 1914-18 had never happened.

This may be one reason why manufacturers like Hayter and Chad Valley made such inroads into the market during this period and a study of their catalogues shows that by 1939 both these companies had eclipsed Raphael Tuck. However, for Tuck's, jigsaw puzzles were always somewhat of a sideline. During the Blitz the factory was destroyed and, though the company established a new factory in Northampton after the war, it never re-started jigsaw production.

Desmond Tuck, the last member of the family to be in the business, retired in 1959. Since then the company has been absorbed in turn by Purnell & Sons, The British Printing Corporation, and is now part of Fine Art Developments.

Chad Valley

Anthony Johnson founded the family business now known as Chad Valley in Birmingham in the early nineteenth century. Its earliest activities were printing, engraving, bookbinding and the production of stationery. In 1860 Anthony's two sons set up their own business and by 1897 one of these sons, Joseph, was running it with his son, Alfred. In 1897 the company moved to a newly built factory in the country village of Harborne outside Birmingham. A small stream, The Chad, flowed nearby and the factory was named the Chad Valley Works. The business traded as Johnson Bros. (Harborne) Ltd. and in addition to stationery produced a range of cardboard games.

Up to 1914 the range of cardboard games and simple toys was extended year by year. The First World War gave a great impetus to the company as imports of games and toys ceased. In 1919 the Harborne Village Institute building was acquired and used to produce boxes and labels for the products. Soon after, space became available at Harborne for the production of jigsaw puzzles and a cutting shop was established. Down one side of the factory two dozen men were employed at saws, and working opposite them were women assembling and checking the puzzles, boxing them, sealing the boxes and enclosing a checker's certificate (fig.10, p17).

Jigsaw production was an important part of the firm's business during the 1920s and 1930s and in 1931 Chad Valley acquired the old established company of Peacock & Co. Ltd. of London, whose wooden toys became incorporated into the Chad Valley range of products. Premises were built to accommodate the expanding business.

It took Chad Valley some years to improve their puzzles but by the later 1920s the quality was excellent and the puzzles from this period up to 1939 are among the finest ever produced. However, towards the end of the 1930s, Chad Valley were in financial difficulties. In the later 1920s (the years of the Depression) it was easy to find cheap labour but the situation was changing fast by the mid-1930s. Chad Valley would not compromise on quality but instead reduced the number of pieces for some puzzles to make production more economical. During the 1930s Chad Valley produced some excellent jigsaw puzzles depicting the Royal Family and royal occasions and, in 1938, were appointed Toy Makers to her Majesty the Queen.

The company was approached by the Head of Publicity at the Great Western Railway and, in 1924, produced a jigsaw puzzle of the recently constructed locomotive *Caerphilly Castle* which was on show at the Wembley Exhibition (see p66). It was a great success and 78,000 copies were made, though only sold at the cost price of 2s6d. Between 1924 and 1939 Chad Valley produced a million promotional puzzles for the G.W.R. as well as many puzzles for Cunard White Star, The British India Steamship Co., Dunlop (see p72), and several other companies and organisations. Selections of puzzles were also produced for W.H. Smith & Son, and Boots The Chemist.

The Second World War brought a halt to puzzle production and it is interesting to note the company's output during the war years. The woodwork factory produced items ranging from small instrument cases to boxes for gun barrels, from hospital tables to tent poles. Electrical work comprised the manufacture of many kinds of coils, electric starters, auto-pilots etc. Children's clothing was made in the soft toy factory, and charts at the printing works. By arrangement with the government one factory, staffed by the firm's oldest employees, continued the production of a limited number of games and toys, including jigsaw puzzles for military hospitals together with draughts, solitaire, chess and dominoes for use by the Forces all over the world.

After the war Chad Valley faced a double challenge. The war had disrupted all business and the costs of wooden jigsaw puzzle production were prohibitive. The company had experimented with card puzzles but were not able to make the necessary investment in large presses for the manufacture of cardboard puzzles. In the immediate post-war years some wooden puzzles were produced but, by the early 1950s, jigsaw puzzle production had ceased.

Roger Swinbourne Johnson, former Chairman of Chad Valley, has commented of this postwar period:

> 'As time went on the prices gradually increased due to inflation, and the number of pieces in a particular puzzle were reduced accordingly. For example, the 2/6 range of G.W.R. puzzles had 150 pieces instead of 200 pieces. Finally the whole jigsaw puzzle operation became a non-commercial undertaking and we gave them up. There were then only two firms making plywood puzzles – Hayter and Chad Valley – most puzzles were cardboard and therefore cheaper, so they did the bulk business, e.g. the range sold by F.W. Woolworths. Chad Valley did not have a Sheridan Press, so we could not produce cardboard puzzles, and we gave it all up thankfully.'

The Chad Valley Company became a public company in 1950, diversified in the 1950s and, in 1960, celebrated its centenary. As a public company, Chad Valley could not avoid being bought up first by Palitoy and later by General Mills. In 1984 Hasbro acquired the Chad Valley name and, in turn, this passed to United Overseas in 1988 and Woolworth in 1989. Since that date cardboard puzzles have again appeared under the Chad Valley name and the range of pictures and sizes of puzzles available is increasing.

G. Hayter (Victory) and Spear's Games

The story of Gerald Hayter who was born into a Dorset farming family in 1901, is an excellent illustration of the history of jigsaw puzzles during the middle part of the twentieth century. A rather lonely youngster, Gerald's fascination with an oval 100-piece puzzle acquired just before the outbreak of the First World War, encouraged him to buy a fretsaw to cut his own puzzles. On leaving school Gerald became a junior bank clerk earning £1 per week. In order to supplement his income, he produced wooden jigsaw puzzles. His output gradually increased and by 1924, when he married, he was spending many hours in the garden shed which he used as a workshop. As a celebration to mark the end of the Great War, he decided on the brand name, Victory. Throughout the 1920s Gerald Hayter continued to work in the bank while developing his jigsaw business. The garden shed was replaced by a small rented workshop in Oxford Road, Bournemouth, and his wife supervised production until Gerald resigned from the bank in 1932. He then purchased a larger workshop in Palmerston Road, Boscombe.

The earliest known pamphlet advertising Victory puzzles dates from about 1928. The illustrated heading on the folded cream-coloured sheet is the same as the picture on the puzzle boxes – smartly dressed parents with their young daughter between them, sitting at a table, assembling a puzzle. The range of subjects on offer, and the retail prices quoted, suggest the middle-class were targeted as customers.

These first puzzles had no guide pictures and were the forerunners of the later *Art Series, Artistic* and, finally, *Gold Box* puzzles. The puzzles themselves ranged in size from 8ins x 6ins (50 pieces, 1s6d) to 28ins x 22ins (1000 pieces, £1.13s). Initially, the number of pieces in each puzzle was 50, 60, 75, 100; then, rose in increments of 50 up to 500; and finally, in increments of 100 up to 1000. Around one hundred and fifty different pictures were available. Apart from these puzzles the only other products on offer at this point were the map puzzles which would be developed over the years. In the tradition of the earliest wooden jigsaw puzzles these were designed to be assembled in their flat boxes and retailed at 2s6d.

Possibly as a commercial experiment, postcard-sized 20-piece puzzles were also offered, each in a labelled bag, as 'ideal for Christmas dips' and a 'good ordinary selling line'. These retailed at 6d each and were probably directed at Sunday Schools and Youth organisations, as well as shops providing Santa Claus grottos. In the early days, and in many later publications, it was stressed that orders should be placed directly with the factory – wholesalers were not involved.

There was rapid expansion over the next two years until about 1930 and Victory moved their premises to Oxford Road, Bournemouth. Puzzle boxes still had no guide pictures but the picture on the boxes now changed with either a man and two women in evening dress doing a puzzle, or else a mother and her three children.

Subjects during this period were very traditional and often genteel – country scenes, hunting, gardens, seascapes, and interiors with people in period costume. Anything modern and within the likely experience of the puzzle maker seems to have been ignored. In 1929 an interesting series of Dickensian scenes, *The Pickwick Series,* was introduced, maybe in imitation of a similar series by Raphael Tuck (see p63). The 60- and 75-piece puzzles were discontinued and the new *Art Series* puzzles had 80 pieces. Double-sided children's puzzles were also introduced in 1929 but, possibly because of production difficulties, were soon discontinued. For the first time,

guide pictures were now pasted on to the lids of boxes. Educational alphabetical puzzles were also produced as were 'sack puzzles of local views' similar to those produced by J. Salmon. These were designed to replace postcards as a souvenir to send to friends, had 36 pieces and cost 9d.

The sixteen-page catalogue for 1930 shows the company poised for significant growth through the 1930s. The Victory works was tucked in beside Bournemouth station with no possibility for expansion and, in 1931, moved to Palmerston Road, Boscombe, a far more suitable site which became the company's permanent home.

In this period there were three particular ideas guiding the selection of puzzle subjects: a growing interest in contemporary themes gave rise to the best-selling *Topical* and *Popular* series; the growing market for children's and educational puzzles; and the introduction of the *Thematic Series* of puzzles which encouraged the collection of sets.

The publicity material of the 1930s gives some idea of the company's marketing and promotional strategy and its perception of what was important. Interlocking pieces were emphasised and 'whimsies' mentioned as enhancing the attractiveness of the puzzles. Boxes varied in colour and the more expensive were tied with ribbon and covered with cellophane. In the early days Gerald Hayter obtained cheap wood by taking apart old tea chests. In the 1930s, beech plywood was used and there are references to 3-, 4- and even 5-plywood. Pictures came from a variety of sources. Gerald was friendly with the proprietor of Beales, a large store in Bournemouth and, in exchange for puzzles, Beales supplied him with out-of-date calendars which were cut up and used as pictures for puzzles.

The 1938/39 catalogue consisted of fifty-four pages of which forty-five list and describe jigsaw puzzles. The company even produced jigsaw puzzle trays in four different sizes. The following is a list of the different series of puzzles being produced just before the outbreak of war and will show how far the company had come in its development and also help to illustrate what happened to most companies producing jigsaw puzzles during this decade.

Animal Series. Introduced by 1937, with domestic animal scenes.

The Beauty Spot Series. First listed 1932/33, with twenty to thirty puzzles depicting British rural scenes and landscapes.

The Big Value Series. Only 1932/33, with five 'period' pictures which may have been derived from the Beales' surplus calendars.

Cathedral Series. By 1935/36 ten paintings by Alread Bruce were in use and, interestingly, the same pictures were used by Ponda and Valentines for their puzzles.

Children's Play Trays. These had cut-out shapes, including *Farm Yard, Jungle, Dogs* and *Soldiers.*

Jigsaw Puzzle Calendars. 1935/36. A full-size calendar-type picture with a jigsaw puzzle in a tray underneath.

Cut-Out Puzzles. These again were *Farmyard, Jungle, Dogs* and *Soldiers,* but this time with an interlocking jigsaw puzzle edge around the figures.

Educational (ME Series). So called because Macmillan Educational pictures were used. An extensive range was produced by 1939 each with suggestions for classroom activity.

Fairy Tale Series. By 1939 ten puzzles using Anne Rochester drawings. *Flying Boat* and *H.M.S. Warspite Constructional Puzzles*, 1938/39. In these puzzles the subject was cut from thicker wood so that it stood out from the surround, giving a 3-D effect.

Jigsaw Game. Dated late 1939. A set of four puzzles, probably to be used in a race, but no example has been found so it may not have been produced.

Geographical Puzzles (M Series). The ever-popular map puzzles, often cut around countries or counties with interlocking sea frame.

Kiddies Favourite. 1938/39. Three small puzzles packed into one box.

London Views. 1935/36. Ten paintings used to make postcard sized 30-piece puzzles of London scenes.

Nursery Rhyme (NR Series). Very similar to the *Fairy Tale Series.*

Old and Modern London. 1935/36. Twelve 200-piece puzzles of London scenes.

Old Prints. Only one reference in 1937. Twelve puzzles made from classical paintings of old English subjects – perhaps more old calendars?

Picture Book Series. 1932/33. Six 15-piece puzzles together in a special box and by 1938/39 eight puzzles were supplied.

Popular Series. First appeared in 1932/33. Ranging from 40 - 150 pieces with twelve different subjects available at any one time. Subjects were the ever popular domestic scenes, huntsmen, country and harbour scenes, period interiors etc. By 1939 there had been a large selection of puzzles produced.

Religious Series. First listed 1932/33. Forty-four different puzzles of Bible scenes have been established, but there is a surprising reference to '195 different subjects in this series'.

Royal Family Puzzles. From the Proclamation of Edward VIII and the Coronation of George VI and Queen Elizabeth onwards, these puzzles were very popular, and Victory proudly noted that, at the 1937 British Industries Fair, Queen Mary purchased twelve copies of each of the three special coronation puzzles. A puzzle in 1937 showed H.R.H. The Duke of Windsor on horseback and referred to 'a delightful picture of this popular ex-monarch' which was, perhaps, intended for the American market.

Super Cut Puzzles. 1938/39. These puzzles were especially challenging with 60 - 2000 pieces, colour-line cutting and no guide pictures! Boxed in gold, their cut was unlike other standard Victory puzzles, and included whimsies.

Topical Series. In the 1932/33 catalogue these appeared as *Trains and Ships Series* but the range was soon extended to cover aircraft, military scenes etc. Victory was slow to follow Chad Valley's lead with regard to ships and

railways but soon caught up. Coded subjects included aircraft, battleships, docks, flying boats, liners, soldiers and trains. Differently sized puzzles of each subject were produced and liners, such as the Queen Mary and Queen Elizabeth, were frequently featured. In 1935 the *Silver Jubilee Train* was a topical addition.

By the outbreak of the Second World War, Victory had about thirty different series of puzzles on offer, with prices from 6d to 70s. Like all similar producers during the war the company suffered the loss of skilled labour and the shortage of materials. Some series, such as *Religious* and *Cathedrals*, were dropped and others lost the larger puzzles in their range because of a shortage of plywood. The company continued, however, and produced new subjects and even new ranges, and children's puzzles were produced in quantity, perhaps because they were smaller and easier to cut.

Despite the post-war difficulties Victory not only maintained all their pre-war series of puzzles but soon added four more. *Animal Band Puzzles, Domestic Animals, Cut-Out Circus Puzzles* and *The Treasure Ship* were all aimed at the younger puzzlers. Export markets were re-opened and new puzzles were added to the *Map Range* and the *Topical Series*.

After a period of considerable austerity the Coronation of Elizabeth II was an impetus for new and exciting puzzles. Victory produced thirty-five different puzzles with eighteen different subjects depicting the Queen, The Duke of Edinburgh, the Coronation Coach, and soldiers and guards on royal duties. By 1956 a new catalogue with improved artwork announced new additions to the *Topical* and *Popular Series*. A *Western Region Express, The Comet Jetliner*, and *Golden Arrow* were typical subjects while older puzzles were deleted. *Jungle Adventure* and *Ambush* were added to the *Adventure Series* for children. The new liner, *SS United States* joined the repertoire of Constructional Puzzles with the 3-D effect (see p95).

Through the later 1950s, Victory continued to adjust their ranges and subjects and, by 1963, a new series of six 100-piece puzzles, *English Views*, was added to the catalogue. A *Birdwatching* and *Flower Calendar* puzzle was also introduced. We are fortunate that one member of the Hayter family, John Stroud, has preserved its history by maintaining a family archive. At the peak of its production in the 1950s, Victory employed around fifty cutters with a further fifty employed in other departments. By 1967 the catalogue was still detailing new children's puzzles, including floor puzzles, but the decline of adult interest in jigsaw puzzles seems evident. In 1970, Gerald Hayter sold the company to the well-known family firm of toy makers, J.W. Spear & Sons, Ltd. of Enfield.

After 1970, significant changes occurred and some existing trends accelerated. For economic reasons, the new company continued to shift the emphasis from adult to child. The wooden puzzle could not compete with the excellent selection of good quality cardboard puzzles now on the market. The *Topical Series* disappeared, and the *Popular Series* was reduced. *Artistic/Gold Box* puzzles in their distinctive boxes with no guide picture became the main adults' puzzles but were expensive and the range of puzzle sizes was also much reduced.

New topical children's puzzles appeared based on television characters and programmes such as *The Magic Roundabout*. The clear way of dating these post-1970 Victory puzzles is that G.J. Hayter & Co. Ltd., a subsidiary of J.W. Spear, is written on the label of the boxes. One other feature is significant. The traditional Victory puzzle featured a more-or-less square piece with four tab slots connecting with the four surrounding pieces. Now many pieces only had two tabs, connecting the top and bottom or the two sides, which meant that the puzzles were no longer fully interlocking. The change was an attempt to reduce costs by making the cutting process faster.

In the 1980s the range was reduced to the *Gold Box* puzzles, the map puzzles which had always been a mainstay of the company's repertoire, and the children's puzzles which were partly made at Spear's own factory in Enfield. At the end of the 1980s, Spears sold their business and the name Victory as a brand name almost, but not quite, disappeared. Sixty years of significant involvement in the British jigsaw puzzle industry came to an end.

John Waddington & Co.

The firm was founded in 1905 by John Waddington and was first based in Leeds. The company specialised in the manufacture of playing cards and, during the years of the Depression, produced cards for the 'Wills Scheme'. This coupon-trading scheme among tobacco companies ceased by the 1930s but, fortunately for Waddington's, there were by this time improved opportunities for expansion.

Under the capable direction of Norman Watson, there were three key developments. Firstly the production of folding cartons which was to help with other ideas as Waddington's were well equipped to make their own boxes and cartons. Secondly, in late 1934, Norman Watson obtained a licence from Parker Bros., U.S.A. to manufacture *Monopoly* a best seller for Waddington's. Thirdly, in the 1920s, an American company in Long Island, New York, developed a method of making jigsaw puzzles from cardboard which cut production costs to a twentieth and increased the popularity of the puzzle.

In the summer of 1933 Waddington's bought the 'know how' and one or two machines from America and began manufacturing cardboard jigsaw puzzles which were distributed to the toy trade by Louis Marx. The whole output was sold to Woolworth and the rapidly growing demand became difficult to meet. Although the expertise had been obtained from America, early manufacturing difficulties were daunting. Though reproducing and printing the pictures and making the cartons for the puzzles was a normal part of Waddington's production, cutting the puzzle and separating the pieces posed significant problems. The giant Sheridan press required a tremendous amount of pressure and the early trials resulted in the machine head being cracked and the breakage of

some of the thick steel posts which took the strain of the cutting operation. This problem was solved by Sid Benson, a skilled letterpress printer, who prepared the cutting in the same way as making ready a letterpress half-tone print.

Later, however, disagreements took place between Louis Marx and Waddington's. The managing director of Louis Marx feared the demand for jigsaw puzzles would diminish and therefore would not place orders of sufficient size to allow Waddington's a continuous production flow. Waddington's, convinced that jigsaw puzzles were here to stay, decided to market their jigsaw puzzles themselves through the stationery trade.

By 1939 the Waddington catalogue was listing four types of jigsaw puzzle. The *New Circular Jigsaw* priced at 1s was introduced in July of that year. This was hailed as 'The Greatest Achievement in Jigsaw Manufacture' and as 'Entirely new – unique in conception – beautifully produced'. It should be noted that Chad Valley had produced an oval wooden puzzle for the G.W.R. as early as 1926 but, in this case, it had only a single picture of a view across the river to Windsor (see p69). The novelty of the Waddington's puzzle was that the series of pictures were arranged round the circumference of the puzzle, for example, eight scenes showing the development of the merchant ship. Waddington's obtained patent No.830942 for these novel puzzles and the design was numbered 201. Four were produced in 1939 and a further four in the early 1940s (see *Compendium of British Jigsaw Puzzles of the Twentieth Century*).

Second came the *Inspector Hornleigh* series linked to the popular radio programme of the day, and the catalogue claimed these to be '...the most amazing puzzles ever produced. Each jigsaw puzzle contains the story of a thrilling crime, and Inspector Hornleigh's own solution.' They were priced at 1s each and there were eight in the series beginning with *No.1 The Silent Passenger* (see *Compendium of British Jigsaw Puzzles of the Twentieth Century*). The puzzles included a short story in leaflet form providing the plot and clues and the jigsaw had to be completed in order to solve the mystery. A solution was included which was impregnated with invisible ink on blue paper which had to be moistened to yield the correct answer. These puzzles were real period pieces and forerunners of the later *Cluedo* puzzles and *Murder She Wrote* and *Taggart*.

Third was the *Waddington Giant Jigsaw* – 'the most delightful puzzles on the market. The largest interlocking cardboard jigsaw ever produced, 439 pieces'. These were 21ins x 15ins and listed as *Vol.1 Irish Castle; Vol.2 The Change at the Chequers; Vol.3 A Welcome Drink; Vol.4 Halt at the Smithy*. Most striking was the large book-shaped, bright red and yellow box. The spine had *Vol.1 IRISH CASTLE 1/-* written on it, and the box was designed to stack on a shelf like a book – as did the early Chad Valley boxes.

Last in the catalogue were the 6d jigsaw puzzles. These also came in the book-shaped boxes with lettering and titles similar to the giant puzzles. One series was called

Waddington's Interlocking Jigsaw Puzzle, 6d and another the *Young People's Jigsaw*, 6d, *Fully Interlocking*. The children's puzzles had larger pieces and were easier to assemble.

By the mid-1940s, Waddington's had combined their expertise in carton-making and jigsaw puzzles and produced the *Jigsaw Book*. This was described as an 'entirely new idea in Picture Books'. Every story dealt with a subject of great human interest, illustrated by a beautifully printed, fully interlocking jigsaw puzzle of over 150 pieces. A baseboard was supplied which was used either as a foundation for the puzzle or, if folded as explained on the back page, as a box. One such puzzle which shows a group of immaculately clad A.T.S. personnel standing beside their spotless three ton army lorries in a country lane, had about 140 cardboard pieces and measures 37cm x 15cm and was probably No.508 (see p76). The box, when made up according to the four-stage process was small and inclined to leak pieces but was, however, a novel and clever idea. Volume 5 consisted of No.509 *The Judgement of Paris* and No.510 *Perseus and Andromeda* – 'Two stories, 1/9, two jigsaws'.

In 1955/56 Waddington's produced their first 1000-piece jigsaw puzzle on 'extra thick board' and the decade saw a large increase in the titles offered, including the well-established circular puzzles. An advertisement in *Everybody's Magazine* in 1957 catches the mood:

'Can you resist helping to make a jigsaw puzzle? Not if it's a WADDINGTON JIGSAW. They are made with every care, DELIGHTFUL DESIGNS, BRILLIANT COLOURINGS, FULLY INTERLOCKING, TASTEFULLY BOXED. Silence is truly golden with Waddington's jigsaws. A charming range from 1/9 to 5/6.'

In the 1960s there were two important developments. The move, in 1964, to the present factory on the south east side of Leeds gave Waddington's plenty of space to create a modern factory in attractive surroundings and also to allow for a future expansion of facilities. Secondly, at the end of the 1960s, Waddington's bought larger Sheridan presses. Nearly thirty years later these are still in use and are the largest presses used by the industry. This development not only enabled the company to cut larger puzzles but, because of the increased power of the press, also improved quality. Production speeded up, a greater volume of puzzles was produced and the range expanded.

By the early 1970s, Waddington's were producing an annual catalogue of their range of puzzles and, from 1971 to 1976, an autumn supplement to the catalogue was also offered to whet the pre-Christmas appetite. Puzzle subjects were, on the whole, traditional – scenic views, reproductions of Old Masters, children, animals; and cartoon characters for the children's puzzles as well as educational maps.

In the early 1980s, the interest in old types of transport was catered for with old-fashioned farm machinery, vintage cars and steam trains. The latter did not appear until 1984 with, appropriately, *Stephenson's Rocket*. The cover of the 1987 catalogue featured the painting *Welcome Home* depicting a nineteenth-century liner in Cunard colours, with single funnel, three masts, two with crossed yards – a rather strange vessel. By this date there were 4000- as well as 3000- and 2000-piece puzzles in the range. Also included were the Cuneo Postage Stamp pictures of four famous trains, and Prince Charles and Princess Diana were featured in glamorous evening dress. Waddington's were also producing hand-cut wooden children's puzzles as well as thick cardboard and wooden tray puzzles.

By the end of the 1980s more contemporary puzzles were added to the range – *Rally Super Cars*, *Racers*, *American Football*, *Combat Aircraft* and *Dinosaurs* – some of these for children. Circular puzzles continued to be an important feature and the 1990 catalogue included a *Wildlife Series* as well as some very challenging puzzles. The Don Breckon series of railway puzzles appeared and also of interest were the four wooden laser-cut puzzles but, by 1991, these had been discontinued as Waddington's felt the quality was unsatisfactory. Other wooden puzzles had also been withdrawn by this time.

New subjects were in the 1992 catalogue and a wide range of children's puzzles especially a large Walt Disney selection which featured scenes from their latest films as well as old favourites like *Mickey Mouse*.

The jigsaw puzzle range, half adults' and half children's, took up 70 pages of the company's 1994 catalogue. Subjects were ever-more varied and challenging with the odd unusual puzzle (No.12427, 750-piece) depicting Princess Diana with three white horses.

Waddington's set up a new factory in 1996 and the cover for that year's catalogue shows the new *3-D Puzz Series* with a young lady putting the finishing touches to Big Ben. 3-D puzzles joined exciting and challenging items making a varied and attractive range of puzzles.

Tower Press

Tower Press was founded in the 1930s by Hans Ehrlich, a refugee from Germany, and his partner Bernard Saalheimer. Initially, the company produced cardboard items such as children's picture books, and probably began jigsaw puzzle production just before the outbreak of war. For a period, Hans Ehrlich was interned on the Isle of Man and there met fellow internee Wilhelm Jondorf, who, before coming to England in 1938, had manufactured greetings cards in Germany. Jondorf had been permitted entry to England as he had access to sufficient money to establish a business in a 'distressed area' in Treforrest, South Wales. After the war he sold the business to Hans Ehrlich who invited Jondorf's son, Harry, to join the new company in 1948.

During this period jigsaw puzzles were pressed out by a sub-contractor, Fordham & Co., in Tottenham, London, using a fairly primitive and unsuitable German embossing press. In fact, the early examples of the 400-piece puzzles (cost 2s9$^{1}/_{2}$d) in the series Nos.111-114, *Cars Old and New* etc., had to be guillotined through the middle and then each half pressed out separately. These 'half puzzles' indicate the exact size of the press. The boxes were attractively printed but poorly designed and pieces were easily lost from either end of the box.

At this time trade was wholesale to four main outlets, Woolworth, British Home Stores, W.H. Smith, and Boots. The company established lasting links with these retailers and, in fact, the first 500-piece puzzle produced was a Regency puzzle especially made for the B.H.S. The box had a central picture with a purple surround, and Harry Jondorf remembers that during the printing process the colour ran giving the picture a dreadful purple hue! Because of the larger pictures needed for the bigger puzzles, printing was difficult and the colours at the edges of the picture were often out of focus.

Tower Press had a warehouse and factory in Westbourne Grove, Kensington Gardens. Fred Miller, a colourful personality, was the company's Art Director and the long running *Good Companions Series* is a good example of the variety and quality of the puzzles produced under his direction. Increasingly, Tower Press concentrated on the production of jigsaw puzzles with their only real competition from Waddington's at Leeds and it is interesting that these puzzles often did not bear the manufacturer's name.

Bernard Saalheimer retired in 1952 and rather surprisingly, Alfred Esterman, a chief buyer at the British Home Stores, became joint Managing Director of the company. Feeling it was moving in the wrong direction, Harry Jondorf left the firm. In 1955 Hans Ehrlich became ill and when, in the following year, Alfred Esterman died the firm was taken over by S. Guiterman and managed by Julius Trup.

Between the 1950s and 1970s, Tower Press employed another sub-contractor, N. Wilkes and Co. to produce their wooden jigsaw puzzles. This company was eventually taken over by Condor, and then by Michael Stanfield and later became part of the Ravensburger Group.

Through the later 1950s Tower Press continued to produce a good range of both cardboard and wooden jigsaw puzzles and in the early 1960s moved to new premises in Walthamstow. Harry Jondorf rejoined the firm in 1961 and with Fred Miller and Sales Director, George Fryer, ran the company within the Guiterman Group. Around this time their sub-contractor, Fordhams, obtained their first Samco Press which was a great development in efficient production.

In 1965, Harry Jondorf, Fred Miller and George Fryer began a new venture. They left Tower Press which continued with its jigsaw production for a further four years until, in 1969, the company ceased trading and was purchased from the Receiver by Waddington's.

During their long period of production Tower Press greatly developed the range and quality of cardboard puzzles and made a significant contribution to the industry. Their series names included: *Good Companions, Beverley, Conway, Embassy, Grand, Haven, Lyric, Mercury, Sceptre, Terminus, Valour, Voyager* and *Walmer*.

Arrow Games

On leaving Tower Press in 1965, Fred Miller, Harry Jondorf and George Fryer acquired a small factory in Waltham Abbey and established a new jigsaw puzzle manufacturing company, Arrow Games. Between them they could only raise around twenty percent of the necessary finance and Lines Bros. provided the additional financial backing. Already experienced in the toy industry, Moray Lines, chairman of Lines Bros., gave considerable help to the newly founded company.

Sub-contractors manufactured the puzzles; the cardboard ones were made by Gasmans of Dagenham and, as they had for Tower Press, N. Wilkes produced the wooden puzzles. Gasmans had one of the TG 42 Samco presses and this, together with the expertise of the three co-founders, ensured the success of the enterprise. The puzzles were of excellent quality in sturdy boxes with lift-off lids, and sold well.

Demand soon outstripped production and the firm acquired another company, Langfords in Birmingham. This factory initially produced cardboard puzzles using an ageing Sheridan press which, although it could cut 1000-piece puzzles in one operation, had long-standing problems with its feed system. The company engineer installed a new feed system at the then enormous cost of £3000. Unfortunately the new feeder proved too much for the press to cope with, the press broke down almost immediately, never to function again and, in 1966, it had to be sold off as scrap.

Meanwhile Tower Press were producing their 2000-piece puzzles and Arrow responded to the challenge by first producing 3000- and, finally, 4000-piece puzzles. In about 1968 the firm moved to West Road, Tottenham to a huge factory, part warehouse and part manufacturing plant, and Samco presses were purchased to manufacture cardboard puzzles. By an extraordinary coincidence, on the day that Arrow Games opened the new factory the old Fordham factory across the road closed. Arrow bought the redundant equipment and took on the staff as well and by 1969 the new manufacturing process was fully operational.

Arrow continued to build up its range with popular series such as the *Age of Steam*. Nevertheless, in 1972, Harry Jondorf was informed that the parent company was going into immediate liquidation. There were difficulties with the bank, to whom Arrow owed a considerable sum, but these were eventually resolved and Milton Bradley, the American toy and games manufacturer, ultimately bought a 75% shareholding while Harry Jondorf and two others held the remainder. Fred Miller, the art director, retired after many years service to the industry.

Harry Jondorf brought in Peter Adby who had been part of the Disney operation and Milton Bradley invested heavily in the company. However, the philosophy of the American company was at odds with Harry and his colleagues and in 1976, following a disagreement, Jondorf and Peter Adby left the company. Milton Bradley was offered premises in Waterford, Eire, at advantageous rates and closed the Tottenham factory, moving all the machinery and contents to the new site.

Arrow continued to produce cardboard jigsaw puzzles until 1987. The company made an important contribution to the continuing development of the cardboard puzzle, enhancing its quality and offering subjects which appealed to collectors.

Falcon Games

In the summer of 1976, Harry Jondorf found himself without a job but with some capital and a lifetime of expertise and experience. He and Peter Adby set up a new company, Falcon Games. At first this was run from Harry's spare bedroom and sub-contractors did all the cutting and pressing of the puzzles. Peter was responsible for design, Harry for marketing and Ted Hurst, also from Arrow, joined the company to manage exports. The spare bedroom was soon replaced by an office in Hatfield and negotiations began for a lease on a factory premises. The following year Falcon bought the entire industrial estate and paid off the mortgage some three years later.

In 1977 Milton Bradley's machinery at their plant in Ireland went up for sale and was bought by Harry. Thus, the Samco presses and other jigsaw puzzle machinery, much of which had originally been designed by Jondorf, returned to the Hatfield factory in the United Kingdom.

By 1978 Falcon had expanded and were exporting to forty countries around the world, with a large market in south east Asia. In the United Kingdom they were the largest suppliers of jigsaws to the Toys-R-Us chain, as well as other retailers. Their largest cardboard puzzle had 5000 pieces.

Throughout this period, Falcon also produced children's wooden puzzles, stamping them out of 3mm Spanish Poplar which is quite a soft wood. However, the quality of the wood gradually declined and Falcon moved production of wooden puzzles to W.J. Trowsdale and Son at Alfreton where children's puzzles were handcut by traditional methods using Russian Birch 6mm plywood. In a very short time Falcon had regained their position as top of the market, high-quality manufacturers and continued to expand and flourish. Their range of adults' cardboard puzzles included many traditional and innovative subjects and quality was excellent.

In January 1996, after nearly fifty years in the industry, Harry Jondorf retired and Falcon was sold to an old established Dutch firm, Hausemann and Hotte. Sadly, yet another well-established jigsaw manufacturing company had passed out of British ownership though excellent quality cardboard puzzles were still produced from its premises at Hatfield. Falcon can take much credit for the widespread success of the industry at the end of the twentieth century.

J. Salmon & Co. Ltd.

J. Salmon & Co. Ltd., originally a Fine Art publisher, was founded in 1880 by the great-grandfather of the present directors. In 1920, J. Salmon anticipated the popularity of puzzles and set up production facilities for wooden jigsaw puzzles which were marketed under the series name of Academy. Cutting was by treadle jigsaws and up to thirty cutters were employed. Salmon developed their range over the coming years and, again, predicted public demand by producing a large number of traditional puzzles – landscapes, hunting and rural scenes, animals and buildings – as well as more contemporary subjects including the latest aircraft, trains and ships. They commissioned artists to produce original pictures in addition to the use of photographs and reproductions of famous paintings.

The quality of the puzzles and boxes was excellent. Early examples had *The Academy Jigsaw Puzzle* on the lid together with 'a charming watercolour in 200 pieces' or some similar description, and a small guide picture and the title of the puzzle on the side of the lid. Later puzzles, such as that of the *Queen Mary*, had a large guide picture on the lid, above a panel with the statistics of the new liner. A shield-shaped label with 'Academy' jigsaw puzzle was in one corner and the puzzle's title, size, number of pieces and price was printed on the end of the lid. In the mid-1930s the company listed the complete range, sizes and prices of its puzzles on the bottom of the box. At 3s6d for a 250-piece puzzle it compared favourably with Victory and Chad Valley.

J. Salmon, like other companies, had to discontinue jigsaw production during the Second World War but, under the guidance of Derek Salmon a grandson of the founder, production re-started in 1946. The range of subjects was, of necessity, reduced but J. Salmon continued to produce wooden puzzles until, in the late-1950s, it could no longer compete with the price of cardboard puzzles.

With over 1300 different titles in its jigsaw puzzle range the company made a substantial contribution to the jigsaw puzzle scene over a period of about forty years. Unusually, the company remained at its premises at 100 London Road, Sevenoaks, Kent, for the entire century. It continues to trade as a Fine Art Publisher from these same premises and is still a family business.

Seddon Packaging and Printing.

Although Seddon Packaging and Printing never actually published puzzles they had a long involvement in the jigsaw puzzle industry. Founded in 1890 by the grandfather of Richard Seddon, the present managing director, it specialised in making items for the shoe trade. In the 1930s Seddon's moved to Kettering and into its present premises after the Second World War.

The company began working in the jigsaw puzzle industry in the 1960s, cutting wooden puzzles for Tower Press. When Harry Jondorf and others left Tower Press and founded Arrow Games they employed Seddons to make their wooden range of puzzles. In 1978 Falcon Games was founded and Seddon's was asked to produce cardboard puzzles. The firm invested in Samco Presses and produced the Falcon range of puzzles until the company was sold in 1996. During this period Seddon's also manufactured puzzles for other companies.

Seddons have a very impressive factory combining the printing, packaging and pressing of jigsaw puzzles. Presses built by Hawks Technical and Bobst of Switzerland, joined the Samco presses to give a large production capacity and their work is of excellent quality. In addition they have all the production facilities and expertise for box making. The only work they do not undertake themselves is making the forms, which is done by Crossland Cutters of Hallesowen.

Because Seddons are available to press puzzles, smaller publishers of cardboard jigsaw puzzles can flourish giving variety to the range of puzzles available.

H.P. Gibson & Sons Ltd.

H.P. Gibson & Sons Ltd., who make Gibson's Games, was established in 1919 and situated in Bishopsgate. In 1940 the premises were bombed and the firm moved to Oxford Street in the 1950s, to Wimbledon in 1979, and to the present site at Greenlea Park in 1983.

The company introduced its range of cardboard jigsaw puzzles in 1986, with the *Britain from the Air* series, producing a total of twenty subjects. In 1993 they introduced six *Wildlife* puzzles and six *Impressionists* puzzles and, in 1994, the six *Classic Interior* puzzles. In 1995 nine *Heritage* puzzles with a wide variety of subjects were added and in 1996 another seven titles, two for circular puzzles, were produced with, again, a diversity of interesting subjects.

Gibson's have standardised their puzzle size at 1000 pieces and particularly rely on the nostalgic appeal of the picture. In 1997 the company will produce both 500- and 1000-piece puzzles featuring Cadbury's and Fry's advertisements from the past.

Gibson's are developing a comprehensive range of puzzles and export to Europe and the United States Their pictures are usually either derived from photographs as with the *Britain from the Air Series*, or from reproductions of paintings but they also commission their own artists to produce original pictures.

Handley Printers

Handley Printers was founded in 1972 by John and Roger Handley who still own and run the company. They have moved from the original premises in Offerton to the present factory in Stockport Road West, Bredbury, on the eastern fringe of Manchester.

Handley Printers began jigsaw puzzle production in 1976 and are important as they and Waddington's are the only companies to produce cardboard puzzles from start to finish. Handley have used two different names over the years, beginning as Handley Printers and then changing to J.R. Puzzles. They took over the smaller company of Inghan Day and also press puzzles for other publishers.

The company obtain their pictures from photographs and prints and also commission work from artists. Their board is imported and glueing is by traditional machine method. The puzzles are pressed on Samco presses and the form-making is done by an outside specialist firm. Box wraps are printed on the premises and J.R. Puzzles are marketed through the normal retail channels.

The company produce a selection of 15- to 500-piece children's puzzles including maps, traditional subjects, television cartoon characters and wildlife. Their adults' puzzles range from 300 to 2000 pieces and have traditional themes: scenic views from home and abroad; Old Masters; vintage cars; sailing ships and steam trains. There is a series of four Edwardian puzzles using sepia photographs of shops and street scenes, and wildlife circular puzzles which, perhaps, owe something to Waddington's. The quality of the puzzles is good and the boxes are attractive. Jigsaw puzzles account for about half of the company's production and are exported to Europe and America. The company employs forty-five people and has a promising future, and such a small, independent company is a rarity in today's cardboard puzzle industry.

Puzzleplex

The Stocken family have been cutting wooden jigsaw puzzles for three generations. Enid Stocken cut her first jigsaw puzzle in 1915 to help raise money for comforts for soldiers wounded in the 1914-18 war and continued until her death in 1983 – her puzzles are now collector's items. Her son Peter, who founded the present firm, learned his skills from her, developed them and has, in turn, taught his four children the art of cutting.

Puzzleplex operate from a building adjacent to a restored farmhouse in Stubbs Walden, deep in rural Yorkshire. There, in the workshop, three treadle jigsaws keep company with a more modern powered-machine and it is clear that the inherited skill of the cutters together with their flair for design combine to produce exquisite and challenging wooden jigsaw puzzles.

This exclusively mail order company specialises in commissioned puzzles and has a mailing list of over 1000. Pictures are mainly traditional and often the customer's own choice. The cutting is distinctive, each family member has their own style, and specialises in whimsies and puzzles with written Valentine or anniversary messages. Rural scenes predominate as these readily lend themselves to the style of cutting and there is always a selection of puzzles in stock which range from 200 to 2250 pieces. Special jigsaws include very cleverly shaped mosaics and also a wide range of beautifully finished three-dimensional puzzles in distinctive woods. This company, like Stave in the United States, has plenty of customers who appreciate its personally tailored products.

Gee Graphite & Jigsaw Dimensions

Based in Mirfield, West Yorkshire, Gee Graphite was founded in 1989 by Colin Gee and the company's jigsaw puzzle production managed by Pauline, his wife, is a sideline to the water-jet industrial cutting operation which is the company's main activity.

In this manufacturing process it is the combination of computer and cutting jet and the capacity to cut many different materials which is so interesting for the future. The company specialises in commissioned puzzles particularly for industry, and the ability to cut such a large variety of materials creates many intriguing possibilities. Gee Graphite have demonstrated the secret of interchangeable pieces on a jigsaw tablemat – the finished mat can either be circular if using all the pieces, or rugby ball-shaped if omitting three of the pieces. Currently, the repertoire of puzzles is small but looks set for expansion over the next few years.

Robert Longstaff

As a young man Robert Longstaff studied biology and physics and also showed an aptitude for woodwork. His talent for making historical musical instruments such as lutes and dulcimers became a time-consuming though not very profitable sideline. While working for the Ministry of Agriculture Robert and his wife, Yvonne, bought a property in Longworth village and established a sanctuary for threatened species of ducks and geese and, also, a craft workshop. In about 1980 he began making dolls' houses, miniature furniture and simple children's toys. The demand for these enabled him to expand his workshop and increase his staff but high production costs were a problem.

As a physicist Robert was familiar with lasers and was convinced they could be utilised for cutting puzzles. He teamed up with some colleagues from Oxford and his machine, which he largely built himself, is now used to produce a wide range of children's puzzles and fretwork for dolls' furniture etc. As it cuts, the laser makes a small burn mark on the wood but as this is only seen on the edge it does not spoil the picture. When cutting M.D.F. board, a relatively new and, when cut, highly toxic material, the laser seals the cut edge making it safe.

Robert Longstaff's range of children's puzzles with traditional and most attractive pictures include floor puzzles and picture puzzles with removable shapes designed to educate as well as amuse. The company has a number of contracts with retail outlets and also sell directly through craft fairs and their factory shop. One of the most interesting aspects of this firm is their diversity of products, including a lute at the time of my visit – a pleasant reminder of Robert's earlier craft as an instrument maker.

The Wentworth Wooden Jigsaw Co. Ltd.

Kevin Preston's interest in manufacturing wooden jigsaw puzzles was initiated by his ailing mother's love of the hobby and her inability to handle cardboard puzzles' pieces. He believed there was a potential demand for wooden jigsaw puzzles which wasn't being met and, after some investigation, felt that this was because of the prohibitive costs of cutting wooden puzzles in the traditional way. He invested in a laser cutter and established a factory at Pinkney, west of Malmesbury.

Kevin and his wife made 40-, 75-, 140-, 250-, and 425-piece adults' wooden jigsaws in five sizes and found that a small run could be economically produced – even individual puzzles when commissioned – in contrast to cardboard puzzles which needed a run of thousands to be viable. He also recognised that there would always be a demand from tourists and that the major tourist

fig.21. From left, John Snoxall, Kevin Preston and David Rossant with the Wentworth Wooden Jigsaw Co.'s laser cutter.

attractions such as the Tower of London would be excellent outlets for his puzzles.

Wentworth wooden puzzles are attractively produced with a very challenging cut including whimsies. The puzzles are designed by Kevin, and the design is transferred via computer to the laser cutter and can easily be stored for future use (fig.21). Special designs with appropriate whimsies for riders, golfers, sailors etc., have been produced. Their 425-piece *Champion Challenge* puzzle is as challenging as any wooden puzzle I have assembled.

Wentworth puzzles are of good quality and the pieces are pleasant to assemble. They have a slightly looser fit than that obtained with a fine-bladed traditional jigsaw, so delicately cut shapes are less likely to get broken. Subjects are traditional: wild animals and birds; steam trains; vintage cars; military; and reproductions of famous paintings. Puzzles are also produced for a large number of tourist attractions. The pieces are contained in cloth bags which are then boxed in smart and durable traditional boxes which either can be stacked flat or as books on a shelf.

W.J. Trowsdale & Son

After an association with Willis in Luton, John Trowsdale founded his own company in 1974 in Alfreton, Derbyshire. His son, Tony, joined him and the business is very much a family concern. The company produces educational puzzles for children, with contracts to supply leading retailers such as Galts, and does not make adults' puzzles.

Trowsdale commission three artists to produce their pictures and the entire production, using traditional methods, takes place on the premises. The pictures are mounted on plywood and trimmed and cutting is done using the renowned 'Hobbies' industrial jigsaw which is now obsolete so that John and Tony have to undertake the service and repairs. Because of its flexibility, the saw is kinder on blades and puzzles can be stack-cut to improve the pace of production and so keep costs down.

When cut, puzzles are checked, sanded and then boxed. The company employs about twenty people and, in addition to the home market, exports puzzles to Sweden, Australia and the United States.

The smallest children's puzzles (4- or 6-piece) compare very favourably in price and quality with the equivalent cardboard puzzles but should Trowsdale wish to produce puzzles with a greater number of pieces, it is difficult to see how they could compete with those companies using laser cutters.

W.R. Kelly Jigsaw Puzzles

W.R. Kelly began making children's wooden jigsaws in London in 1949, moved to Luton and then, in 1963, to Stonham Aspall in Suffolk. At first, the company produced its puzzles in the cottage and annexe across the road from the present factory then gradually expanded to a larger building. A family concern, the company was the main supplier for Willis Toys at Saffron Walden and in 1978, when the Kelly's felt ready to retire, the business was sold to Mr. Willis whose son ran the Saffron Walden company. Mr Willis senior, though well into his eighties, still presides over the Stonham factory .

In addition to its children's puzzles W.R. Kelly is, to my knowledge, the only factory cutting adults' wooden jigsaw puzzles using traditional methods. Modern, large industrial fretsaws are used and, with a coarse blade, eight puzzles can be stack-cut. The actual cut is a simple one, though quite challenging to assemble, and each cutter can cut eight 200-piece puzzles in about an hour – an impressive rate.

The company has used Finnish Birch but found this too hard on the saw blades so now uses 4mm or 6mm Italian Poplar plywood. Interestingly, most companies using lasers prefer the Finnish Birch because its darker colour disguises the burn mark of the laser. Puzzles range from just 4 to 80 pieces with a wide variety of subjects.

James Hamilton

While on holiday in the Seychelles, Gordon McGee produced a cassette tape of *Island Sounds* to sell to the tourists. This was a great success and one of his agents suggested that a jigsaw puzzle of the Seychelles might also prove popular. On his return to England, Gordon found a firm to stamp the puzzle, and commissioned a picture of the Seychelles, *The Coral Reef*, which was very successful and is still in production.

The company was founded in 1981 as James Hamilton, and since then has built up a strong business specialising in colourful and challenging wildlife puzzles of both British and overseas scenes. Puzzles have been produced for the Royal Society for the Protection of Birds, The World Wildlife Fund, The National Trust, and for export.

The company has increased their range and adults' puzzles are produced in five sizes, from 500 to 2000 pieces, and there is a range of 70-piece puzzles for children. An excellent catalogue and mail order facility is offered.

George Luck

George Luck founded his present company at Bower Hinton, Somerset, in about 1977, and the small factory is beautifully situated among the trees and shrubs of his large garden. With eight cutters using traditional jigsaws, and a staff of about twenty, he produces high-quality children's

wooden jigsaw puzzles designed by Kay Luck and Philip Gell. The company has produced a total of five hundred designs with around two hundred currently in production.

Among the very interesting designs produced are two- and three-layered puzzles, hand-painted to a very high standard, and also map puzzles in which the different counties or countries are represented by the shapes of appropriate animals (see p110).

The company received a Design Award in 1982 and export a large proportion of its products to America, Japan and Germany, where there is a demand for puzzles of such good quality.

Above: fig.22. Chad Valley catalogue, 1935.

Left and below: figs.23 and 24. The original uncut Chad Valley puzzle prints (see fig.22).

CHAPTER 6

THE AMATEUR JIGSAW PUZZLE MAKER

I would define amateur jigsaw puzzle makers as those who do not attempt to make a living from the manufacture of jigsaw puzzles, though some may have made a profit out of their hobby, and others may make a small charge to cover costs. Almost all amateurs make wooden rather than cardboard puzzles and do not use the larger commercial jigsaws. Beyond this there is not a stereotypical 'amateur', and every permutation of puzzle is to be found. My father made a puzzle in about 1945 using a hand-held fretsaw and a piece of plywood which had been gleaned from some unwanted piece of furniture. It had about 30 semi-interlocking pieces and the picture came from the front of a *Country Life* magazine. When I had assembled it, I discovered that the picture was an early painting by Terence Cuneo (see p73).

During the century the sources for pictures have changed dramatically, ranging from small photographs to a massive 40ft by 10ft Ford poster, and a wide diversity of subjects. Moreover, the advent of the colour photocopying service in many High Streets allows the amateur access to one-off printing facilities which many commercial manufacturers would have envied twenty years ago. The size of pictures can be enlarged or reduced and collages of photographs assembled and copied without damage to the originals, particularly important when using old prints. Such puzzles can make unique and fascinating gifts.

With regard to making puzzles; in my experience top quality plywood is not widely available and I would be reluctant to use my jigsaw on M.D.F. board because of its high glue content and toxic properties. Much plywood consists of very thin, easily splintered outer layers and a centre made of softer wood or even composite material which is entirely unsuitable for delicate work with a jigsaw. So I would recommend seeking out top quality plywood. Amateurs tend to use a variety of glues and have different methods for trimming and sanding. Glue can be applied to an ordinary sized puzzle with a brush but care must be taken to remove air bubbles and to allow the picture to dry completely before cutting begins. Trimming the edges can be done with a modelling knife or scalpel or a piece of fine sandpaper.

The most significant differences in amateur and professional production are the saws and the cutting technique and here the amateur has an advantage. With no deadline or production target the amateur is able to experiment and to develop more varied and intricate cutting techniques. Cutting jigsaw puzzles lends itself to original designs and unusual ideas and puzzles can be tailor made. Cutting names and initials, as well as other appropriate whimsies, into a puzzle is much easier for the amateur. The puzzle can be interlocking or non-interlocking, cut in a straight line or circular mode and so forth and, if he or she wishes, the cutter can imitate the style of one of the famous companies of the past such as Victory or Tuck. Many amateurs develop their own style of whimsies, often elaborate and amusing, and will cut circular puzzles or puzzles with irregular edges.

It is worth selecting a saw which suits your cutting technique. There are a wide variety available including, occasionally, very old treadle ones (see Chapter 4). Most saws have a fairly small table and it is simplest to begin by cutting a larger puzzle into quarters or even eighths. The pieces are then far more manageable on the table. Care must be taken not to cut them too thinly as they may easily break.

Throughout the century many hundreds of people have cut jigsaw puzzles, ranging from parents or grandparents who used hand-held fretsaws to make simple puzzles for children, to those who are ranked among the world's finest cutters of puzzles. Sadly, as most amateurs neglected to put their name, address and the date of cutting on their puzzles there is usually no way of investigating the maker.

It is impossible to classify amateur cutters even when one is able to identify them. However, there are a number who have been distinguished by their skill and artistry and it is perhaps no coincidence that some of the best have cut many of the puzzles for the British Jigsaw Puzzle Library. The Library (see Chapter 7) has always required a supply of wooden puzzles of the highest quality and complexity and has been able to find the best cutters in the land to meet its demand. Beginning with Eric Bond, who cut from 1941 until his death in 1982, the roll includes Enid Stocken, 1951-1983, Eric and Ray Pedley, Dick Sawbridge, Peter Stokes and Mark Armstrong. At present Sara White and Meredith Worsfold supply many of the new puzzles.

Enid Stocken, as already mentioned, cut her first jigsaw puzzles in 1915 in order to raise money for comforts for wounded soldiers and thereby unveiled a talent that might otherwise have remained untapped. Her remarkably accomplished puzzles were to become legendary in her lifetime. A friend and jigsaw connoisseur wrote 'Her style of cutting was interlocking and not very hard, but of unique sunny charm'. Imposed on the picture were skilfully cut, homely little shapes of considerable technical complexity. During her seventy-year period as a cutter she

fig.25. Meredith Worsfold at work.

cut between twenty and twenty-five thousand puzzles, often several during one day, most of which are now the treasured possessions of collectors who continue to enjoy them. No record was kept of all her puzzles, but if you have a beautiful wooden puzzle with a small wheelbarrow whimsy cut in the centre, it is one of Enid's.

Meredith Worsfold developed a great love for puzzles in childhood. In the early 1980s he purchased a Vibro jigsaw and soon supplemented this with a larger machine. A later Hegner saw also sits on the bench in his garden workshop allowing him wide scope in his cutting. Over a period of about fifteen years he has cut around 1350 puzzles for adults and a further 250 for children. Puzzle sizes range from 100 to 1250+ pieces, and subjects include birds and animals; railway and traction engines; cars and aircraft; rural scenes including a series of seasonal pictures of the countryside; and silhouette and double-sided puzzles. He has even cut a 120-piece micro puzzle, three inches square – tweezers and a magnifying glass are needed to assemble it.

Meredith cuts in a conventional manner, without whimsies, and reckons to cut at a very fast 100 pieces an hour. He has commissioned attractive and sturdy boxes for his puzzles as he feels a good puzzle deserves a good, safe box. One of the most talented cutters working in the last two decades of the century, Meredith has resolutely refused to over-commit himself and turn a most enjoyable hobby into a burden. He keeps a complete record of every one of his puzzles (fig.25).

Sara White has had a fascination for jigsaw puzzles since childhood but her real involvement began in about 1981 when her husband Paul, a skilled engineer with a talent for resurrecting machinery, found an old Hobbies treadle jigsaw on a scrap heap. He brought it home, got it into working order and Sara set to work cutting puzzles. Later in the 1980s Hayters, the makers of Victory puzzles, ceased trading and Sara was able to acquire from them some beautiful prints ideal for jigsaw puzzles, and Paul rescued a thirty inch jigsaw for cutting the larger puzzles. She has now moved on to an electric jigsaw for her work which allows her extra speed in cutting.

Sara has developed an intricate cut, which often baffles with the totally unexpected. This, combined with clever line cutting and her eye for an attractive picture means that her large jigsaws, often up to 1250 pieces, are a genuine challenge. One of her specialities is the positioning of whimsies – a cat curled up on a window sill, a dog with its paws against a tree while a squirrel scurries away up above it. These add a new dimension to the puzzles and Sara will personalise whimsies as well. A magnificent 1050-piece wooden puzzle of birds has thirty-four easily recognisable different breeds of English dogs concealed within it and the way they are disguised is ingenious (see p124). Sara is one of the many cutters who has found that wrapping paper often makes an attractive picture for a puzzle.

Throughout the United Kingdom, there are many amateur cutters creating a wide variety of puzzles and using every kind of technique and subterfuge to puzzle others. The wide availability of a good range of electric jigsaws has made this possible and developments in the future are likely to increase the scope for amateurs.

It should again be stressed that this involvement of amateurs in the jigsaw industry and their relatively large contribution is a very important dimension of the whole jigsaw puzzle scene in Britain today.

CHAPTER 7

JIGSAW LIBRARIES, CLUBS AND SOCIETIES

In the early days of the twentieth century, books, games and jigsaw puzzles were a main source of indoor leisure activity. Books and jigsaw puzzles had one thing in common – many people would want to read or assemble them once only. However, there was an important difference. In 1925, excellent books could be bought for one to two shillings. There was even the 1d dreadful! Few good-sized adults' jigsaw puzzles sold for less than five shillings so it was not surprising that, following the example of book libraries, jigsaw puzzle libraries and clubs came into existence.

For most enthusiasts the appeal of the jigsaw puzzle lay in its challenge. Once the puzzle was assembled and the challenge conquered most people lost interest in the puzzle though they may have had a few old favourites. Often, however, they liked to be able to exchange the completed puzzle for another and this was the role for the libraries. The library or club would seek to build up a large stock of difficult, wooden puzzles in special boxes without, as a rule, guide pictures. Members paid a yearly subscription and then a borrowing fee plus the cost of postage and, usually, there was no limit to the number of puzzles a member could borrow during the year.

It is difficult to estimate exactly how many of these clubs and libraries existed. Puzzles from the A.1. Jigsaw Club have appeared in large numbers indicating that it was a sizeable and long-running library and puzzles have also surfaced from the Original Jigsaw Puzzle Club, London, Miss Rutherford's Club, Liverpool, and from clubs in Torquay, Bexhill, and Worthing. However, many of the puzzle clubs were small and I suspect that a large number flourished in the 1920s and 1930s before the impact of the cardboard puzzle diminished demand.

However, some clubs flourished at a later date. Founded by Dolly MacDougall in Framlingham in 1957, the East Anglian Jigsaw Club was later taken over by her grandson, Andrew Kershaw, and based in St. Albans. The puzzles were wooden and sent out in plastic bags as boxes were too bulky and easily damaged in the post. Many of the puzzles were cut either by Dolly or Andrew and the club had about seventy members living as far away as Cornwall, Liverpool and Grimsby. It closed in 1969.

The British Jigsaw Puzzle Club is the one long-established club which continues to thrive. Carolyn Beves ran the club for seventeen years and, as the club was typical of so many of the time, I think it interesting to include the following summary of her written account of its history.

In the autumn of 1932, the Hon. James Craig of Stormont Castle and 39 Markham Street, London, and his twin brother, sons of the first Prime Minister of Northern Ireland, took the lease of a small room in 169 Sloane Street intending to 'use the room as an office in connection with a Jigsaw Puzzle Club'. It appears that the brothers had a great passion for puzzles and games of all kinds, and saw the Jigsaw Club as a means of setting up a collection of jigsaw puzzles for the use of themselves and their friends. By early 1933 the club was in operation and owned puzzles by Tuck, Chandos, Chad Valley and Holtzapffel.

fig.26. Elsie Baldwin and Peter Grimes.

An early member, Mrs. Rachael Lawrence, took responsibility for running the club in 1933 and in January 1935 became its official owner. The club grew and as a mail order service developed, Miss Elsie Baldwin was recruited at £1.50 per week to do the clerical work. Enclosed in each puzzle box was a booklet inviting members to record comments, and as a check that the puzzle was complete. Over the years these booklets have given an invaluable record of both puzzles and members, and the likes and dislikes of the latter make fascinating reading. The list of rules and conditions of membership has hardly changed in over sixty years. Rachael left London and, in 1942, sold the business to Elsie Baldwin (fig.26).

Elsie, a lively lady who had been a manager and chaperone of troupes of Tiller Girls, added to the club's stock by buying as many Victory jigsaw puzzles as she could afford. Gerald Hayter of Victory became a firm friend and these puzzles were the mainstay of the club though she recruited other cutters to make puzzles, and a friend, Mrs. Whitehead, to make replacement pieces.

The club was open from 11am to 3.30pm. Closing time was strictly adhered to, with pleas and knocks from late members ignored – such rigidity even extended to a formidable ex-Vicereine of India. Press cuttings of the mid-1930s show Elsie Baldwin's pride in her clientele of Members of Parliament, judges, and peers, as well as society ladies and gentlemen. She was an excellent self-publicist, claiming 'hundreds of members and thousands of puzzles' which was certainly an exaggeration. Her successor believed the club probably averaged forty to fifty members and juggled very cleverly with a surprisingly small stock of puzzles. The booklet accompanying a puzzle circulating in the 1930s and 1940s shows it to have been assembled in 1941 by fourteen members with an average number in the 1980s of around four or five. The subscription to the club was £2.50, a figure at which it remained until 1962.

The war proved a very challenging period for the club and press cuttings of that time show the pleasure the jigsaw puzzles brought to members and convalescent troops, as well as the Speaker of the House of Commons and Mr. Attlee. That the club survived was entirely due to Elsie Baldwin's enterprise and commitment.

By the late 1940s an adjoining larger room had been rented. Much to Elsie's delight the Princesses Marie Louise and Helena Victoria became members and she headed her writing paper 'Under Royal Patronage'! In 1951 the Princess Marie Louise introduced an accomplished cutter, Enid Stocken, but nearly bankrupted the club by ordering £60 worth of jigsaws from her – half the total budget. Fortunately, in the long run, the Stocken puzzles proved to be a great asset.

Mrs. Kitty Waterfield was a very active member of the club and when Elsie was injured in a car accident in 1959 agreed to step into the breach. In 1960 she permanently took over its administration, moved the premises to Fulham Road and began modernising the club. Action was taken to obtain new puzzles and have replacement pieces made for old ones. The parcel strike in 1962 could have proved disastrous for the club but Dorothy MacMillan, the Prime Minister's wife, lent Kitty a car and driver to continue local deliveries. Gradually, through hard work and perseverance, the club began to thrive again. In 1967 Kitty decided to sell and once again an heir was at hand.

Goldwynne Jones was used to helping Kitty with the general management of the club. She and her sister Nancy took it over, moved it from central London to Croydon, and ran it almost entirely as a postal enterprise. Their brother, Robert, modernised the club's administration. Each member was given a card which recorded the puzzles borrowed, likes and dislikes and any relevant personal details, such as failing sight. Puzzle boxes were relabelled to indicate the name of the cutter, and the degree of difficulty. The subscription was raised to £9 and by 1970 the business was sound and efficient.

fig.27. Brian and Carolyn Beves.

In 1970 Carolyn Beves bought the club and moved it to Blackheath, changing its name to The British Jigsaw Puzzle Library (fig.27). Eric Bond, Enid Stocken and Mr. Lea continued to cut puzzles and Victory cut the Library's own pictures to provide more individual puzzles. Members could borrow more than one puzzle at a time and were allowed a puzzle to bridge the exchange period. Carolyn proved highly skilful at finding new puzzles – 250 Victory's were followed by a collection of 400 puzzles from the 1920s. New cutters included Eric and Roy Pedley, Dick Sawbridge, Peter Stokes and Mark Armstrong. The Library moved into the 1980s successfully recruiting new members, generally through the personal recommendation of existing ones. Carolyn pensioned off the oldest puzzles and increased the stock to 3700. The club's success was due to her flair and hard work and, also, her keen interest in, and affection for, her many members. In response to those who ask 'who joins the Library' Carolyn says:

'Apart from the royal connection, a random selection would have been the postman who delivered the parcels; the journalist who came to record an interview; the social worker who had to have a puzzle as it was 'the only problem I can actually solve'; the handicapped, the insomniac, the overworked executive, the hostess entertaining her house guests.'

A variety of circumstances led to the Library being sold in 1986 to a member, Pearl Crompton, and her husband who moved it to its present site in Leamington Spa. On my visit in 1995, Pearl and Michael showed me their method of operation and their superb stock of puzzles (fig.28). The Library at that date had about 350 members, which seems to be a constant figure, and about 3500 puzzles in circulation. Pearl has found new cutters including Sara White and Meredith Worsfold and commissioned her own puzzles. Each year she packs a very special parcel for the Queen's Christmas house-party at Sandringham. The British Jigsaw Puzzle Library is in very capable and dedicated hands and continues to give many hours of pleasure to its members all over the United Kingdom.

I have included this brief portrait of the club because its history typifies the background and operation of all the other clubs and libraries which were its contemporaries except, where they eventually closed, the British Jigsaw Library has survived and flourished.

In 1994 Christine Manders, of Beccles, Suffolk, established a library in her area with 300 cardboard puzzles. By obtaining grants from local groups and charities she was able to offer a free membership to the housebound and the disabled with the added advantage of home-deliveries. By 1996 the library had sixty members and 1000 puzzles. A small charge is made for each puzzle loaned and the library is also open to members twice a month.

As far as I can tell there has never been a specific society for jigsaw puzzle enthusiasts until the advent of the

fig.28. Pearl Crompton.

Benevolent Confraternity of Dissectologists in October 1985. It took its title from the earliest jigsaw puzzles which were called 'Dissected Maps' and 'Dissected Pictures'. A group of seven met at Norman and Sally Plumridge's house near Guildford – between us we had interests in model railways, antiques, jigsaw puzzles and other collectables, and we spent a very sociable evening assembling jigsaws. We resolved to be Associates of the Benevolent Confraternity of Dissectologists, having decided the initials ABCD would be easy to remember even after a good supper. The annual subscription was set at a very modest £1 and membership cards made in the form of a small jigsaw puzzle with the initial letter of the member's name cut into it, were sent in pieces ready to be assembled. The aims of the society were set out on the membership application form:

1. To promote the interest of jigsaw puzzles.
2. To do some research into the history of jigsaw puzzles and to start a photographic library.
3. To keep members in touch with one another and where possible help to arrange meetings.
4. To circulate newsletters to members on a regular basis.
5. To enjoy doing puzzles.

With four meetings each year, three newsletters, a magazine and an excellent photographic archive of puzzles, the B.C.D. has maintained its objectives. It has attracted members from as far afield as Alaska and California, Australia and New Zealand and has half-a-dozen Dutch members who have founded their own thriving society. In the United Kingdom the society has members from most age groups and from every walk of life. There are assemblers, collectors, cutters, restorers and combinations of all four.

Many members have developed their own interest in a particular make or type of jigsaw puzzle and done much research on their subject. Some of this has been published privately and some is yet to come.

Jigsaw puzzles can be a fairly solitary hobby and not everyone welcomes interlopers 'helping' with their puzzle. At our meetings all the normal rules of puzzle etiquette are waived and everyone attempts each other's puzzle. Moreover, the society enables members to keep contact with one another and, through a separate publication, *Collector's Roundabout*, to buy, sell, and exchange jigsaw puzzles and other items. One feature of the B.C.D. is that its members have preserved so many jigsaw puzzles which would otherwise have perished.

CHAPTER 8

BRITISH JIGSAW PUZZLES IN THE YEAR 2000

During the last hundred years there have been startling developments in the production of jigsaw puzzles. A century ago a small number of manufacturers supplied almost entirely wooden puzzles to the wealthy. Today the local toyshop offers a good quality 500-piece cardboard puzzle for as little as £2. John Spilsbury's invention in 1760 has lost none of its appeal over nearly two and a half centuries.

Current manufacturers fall into three categories. Cardboard puzzle makers, wooden puzzle makers, and those using other materials such as plastic. In addition there are cardboard puzzle manufacturers who make the puzzles from start to finish, those who publish and sell the puzzles, and those who just produce the puzzles.

Sadly Waddington's factory in Leeds closed in 1997 after nearly one hundred years as a family firm producing a number of popular games such as the famed *Monopoly,* and a very diverse range of puzzles. Some unwise product decisions were among the reasons for its closure. Abandoning the development of laser-cut wooden puzzles was certainly short-sighted and Waddington's major financial commitment to the *3D Puzz,* a new, untried variation proved too great a risk (see p112). *3D Puzz* suffered considerable teething troubles in production and also, the 3-D puzzle, by its very nature, is lacking in appeal to the majority of jigsaw enthusiasts who remain loyal to the traditional puzzle. Its American parent company, Hasbro, moved production to Spain and Southern Ireland where it already had plants in operation. One day, surely, a history will be written of the fine company which was Waddington's of Leeds.

Consequently, at the end of 1997 there are only two companies which actually manufacture cardboard puzzles from start to finish. One is Handley Printers of Stockport, Cheshire which markets J.R. Puzzles and has an exciting and expanding range. The other is Rembrandt Games of Watford. This is an interesting firm because, although it has been in business for well over twenty years, first as Pleasure Toys Ltd., and later as Castile Games, almost all of its considerable output has been marketed through other companies – such as Waddington's – and under other companies' brand names. As a result it is not well-known even though it produces, unusually, both wooden handcut puzzles as well as pressing cardboard ones. With the demise of Waddington's the company has resolved to market an increasing number of puzzles under its own brand name and these will become more widely available in the future.

In addition to Handley Printers and Rembrandt Games other publishers of cardboard puzzles have also extended their range of puzzles, notably James Hamilton of Salisbury and Gibson's Games. Hamilton's have new business opportunities as a result of the closure of Waddington's, and Gibson's Games plan to extend their excellent range of puzzles with twelve new titles in 1998. It is interesting to note how their range specifically caters for the British market with pictures of stately homes, steam railways, vintage cars, thatched cottages and gardens, and old masterpieces. It is doubtful whether any multi-national company could cater to this extent for the British market. However, large numbers of pressed cardboard puzzles are imported into this country especially by Falcon Games (Holland), Robenau Toys [Educa Puzzles] (Spain), Ravensburger (Germany), and Milton Bradley, taking over the Waddington name, (U.S.A. or Eire).

Other producers of cardboard puzzles include Cranham Publications, Orchard Toys, Really Useful Games, B.V. Leisure (who import many of their puzzles), Historical Games and Puzzles, Paul Lamond Games, Cheatwell Games, Mandolin Puzzles, and Moat House Products. These publishers of jigsaw puzzles use other manufacturers to press their puzzles and all are planning expansion of their ranges. When the Dutch firm, Jumbo, bought Falcon Games, Seddon Printing and Packaging had spare capacity and this is already being taken up by the British publishers of puzzles who rely on Seddon's to press their puzzles. The company is well equipped with modern presses which produce puzzles of excellent quality.

The producers of wooden jigsaw puzzles can be divided into those who produce for the adult market and those producing children's puzzles. The latter are by far the larger sector at present as children's puzzles can be produced quite cheaply. The Early Learning Centre, Galt, and Willis Toys as well as smaller companies like Big-Jigs, Tomahawk Toys, and George Luck all market children's puzzles cut by traditional methods. Manufacturing companies such as W.R. Kelly and Trowsdale cut commercial jigsaws and stack-cut up to an impressive eight puzzles at a time.

However, they have to compete with Robert Longstaff at Abingdon, cutting excellent quality children's puzzles with the laser he has developed. Robert has recently been developing adults' 'brain-teaser' puzzles, some, such as his 'stick puzzles', based on designs of antique puzzles. He has also developed a curved design of non-interlocking pieces; puzzles with transferred pieces to baffle those who rely on

fig.29. A Puzzleplex jigsaw puzzle with its characteristic whimsies.

fig.30. Jonathan Stocken.

In addition to the commercial companies, there are 'amateurs' who cut wooden puzzles often of a large size and great complexity. Among these are Peter and Jonathan Stocken of Puzzleplex (figs.29 and 30) Sara White and Dave Cooper. Most puzzles are cut to order with the added bonus of personalised designs and a choice of pictures for the customer. They are of superb quality, very challenging to assemble, and good value for those who want something really special.

Colin Gee is expanding his production capacity for water-jet cutting and is planning to increase his jigsaw puzzle production. Interestingly, his latest puzzle is made of multi-coloured plastic and is used to teach students the composition of DNA in bio-chemistry. So, puzzles have gone full circle and the very latest, as with the first, is an educational aid.

The development of computer-controlled lasers and water-jets for cutting puzzles is so rapid that it is impossible to predict the rate of progress. The design of the puzzle can be varied and modified at the touch of a button and different cuts of the same puzzle can be made by swapping one piece of software for another. Puzzles with fully interchangeable pieces are now being created by computer technology and it is clear that in the future more and more of the design will be done by computer programming.

While the different manufacturers of puzzles develop and flourish there are many other interesting activities taking place which testify to the strength of the hobby. In these last years of the century many enthusiasts have been researching the history of jigsaw puzzles and those with particular collections have compiled lists of the puzzles made in that range, as archive material and old catalogues are virtually non-existent. The results of this research are shown in the supplement to this book which lists jigsaw puzzles produced during the course of this century. The list will continue to grow and I hope other research will be

the grain of the wood for help; and puzzles with interchangeable pieces. These new concepts, which to some extent parallel those of Stave puzzles in the United States, promise much dissectological torture for enthusiasts in the future.

Meanwhile, Optimago continue an excellent range of subjects for adults with their traditionally stack-cut wooden puzzles. They have to contend with the laser-cut puzzles of the Wentworth Wooden Jigsaw Co., who are aiming to produce a larger puzzle than their existing 250- and 425-piece ones, and to extend their repertoire of subjects. There is a large demand for Wentworth's made-to-order range both from individuals and outlets such as stately homes and gardens. This ability to economically produce small orders, even one-off puzzles, fully exploits the advantages of laser cutting.

fig.31. Label from inside a Maids of Kent Craft Shop puzzle box.

published in due course giving more detailed histories of the various companies and their range of puzzles.

As enthusiasts increase their collections so we gain a clearer picture of the history of jigsaw puzzles. For example, a superb puzzle of *Alice in Wonderland* with *Mock Turtle* and *Gryphon* (see cover) was in a box stating that it originated in the 'Maids of Kent Craft Shop' run by Helen Helmore and Vera Tassell who ran a Jigsaw Puzzle Club (fig.31).

In the summer of 1997, the third Isle of Wight Jigsaw Puzzle Festival was held at East Cowes with increased numbers of puzzles, competitions and displays (fig.32). The increasing interest in this festival is another reflection of the hobby's growing popularity. Jigsaw puzzle collectors in various parts of the country take the opportunity to give exhibitions of their puzzles, some raising money for charity. It is an activity with which many people are familiar and during the later 1990s has been featured on radio and television. Jigsaw puzzles have found their way on to the National Curriculum with students seeking resource material for their projects, computer jigsaw games are increasing in number and the hobby now has its place on the Internet.

So the simple concept of the jigsaw puzzle continues to thrive and develop, taking full advantage of modern technology to produce an infinity of variations and complexities to better frustrate and challenge jigsaw puzzle enthusiasts. A repeat of the phenomenal craze of the 1920s and 1930s is unlikely but all the signs are that the hobby will continue to increase steadily in popularity throughout the world. The future is exciting.

fig.32. Isle of Wight Jigsaw Puzzle Festival, 1997.

TURN OF THE CENTURY PUZZLES

Peacock from Children's Animal Puzzle Box, by
E. Nister & E.P. Dunn, London & New York,
printed in Bavaria, 12 pieces, thick cardboard,
c.1905.

Parable of the Sower. Betts, one of a series, 37 pieces, wooden, c.1895.

Five 12-piece puzzles from The *Bible
Picture Book* by E. Nister and
E.P. Dunn, London & New York,
thick cardboard, c.1905.

TURN OF THE CENTURY PUZZLES

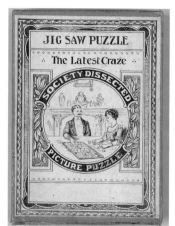

Below: *Always on the Water Wagon*, with its box, left. Retailed by Hamleys, 80 pieces, wooden, c.1905.

Girl Feeding Fowls. Raphael Tuck, distinctive cut, 150 pieces, wooden, c.1900.

Evening Scene. Zig-Zag Puzzle with whimsies, 152 pieces, wooden, c.1905.

The Guardian Angel. Maker unknown, this 300-piece puzzle reflects the changing attitude to boys and butterflies, wooden, c.1906.

HOLTZAPFFEL

Salome dances before Herod. 600 pieces, wooden, c.1905.

Above: *The Charcoal Burners.* Japanese woodcut, 250 pieces, wooden, c.1910.

Right: *The Samurai.* Japanese woodcut, 250 pieces, wooden, c.1910.

HOLTZAPFFEL

Bibby Liner Approaching Rangoon by James S. Mann. Figure-It-Out English Jigsaw Puzzle, 500 pieces, wooden, c.1910.

HOLTZAPFFEL

The Snake Charmer or *Queen Cleopatra*. Figure-It-Out English Jigsaw Puzzle, 450 pieces, wooden, c.1905.

EARLY WOODEN PUZZLES

Dog in the Manger. Zig-Zag Puzzle, 120 pieces, wooden, c.1910.

The Bone of Contention. Salmon Academy, 150 pieces, c.1928.

Guarding the Sheep Fold. Salmon Academy, 300 pieces, c.1935.

In an Italian Homestead. Toys to Teach, 150 pieces, wooden, c.1925.

Fishing Boats. Salmon Academy, 300 pieces, wooden, c.1905.

My Daddy's a Soldier. C. Combridge, 150 pieces, wooden, c.1915.

THE DEVELOPMENT OF BOXES

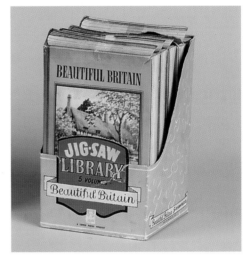

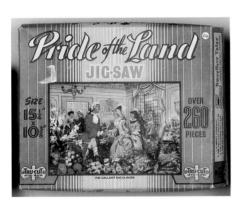

From top, left to right: *The Sower*, Betts, wooden box with sliding lid, c.1900; *Airliner*, Salmon Academy, 1920s; *Coronation Scot*, Victory, 1930s; *The Night Mail*, Chad Valley for G.W.R., 1936; *Waddington Jigsaw Puzzle*, c.1938; *Beautiful Britain*, Tower Press Library, 5 vols, c.1950; *Gallant Encounter*, Tru-Cut, 1950s; *Waterfowl*, Waddington, c.1975; *The Royal Wedding, Prince Charles and Lady Diana*, Arrow, 1000 pieces, 1981; *Ballet Class*, Ravensburger, 1996.

HISTORY AND MONARCHY

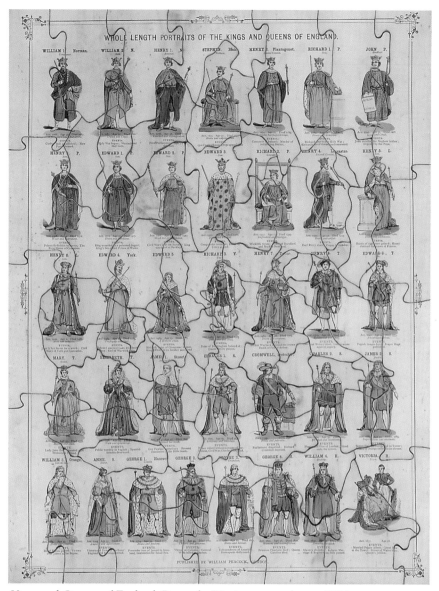

Kings and Queens of England. Peacock, 80 pieces, wooden, c.1900.

King Henry VIII and his Wives. Moat House Puzzles, 750 pieces, cardboard, 1997.

ROYAL PUZZLES

Queen Victoria. Zig-Zag Puzzle, 750 pieces, wooden. The print is c.1900 but the actual puzzle is c.1920.

ROYAL PUZZLES

Jubilee Group 1935. Chad Valley, 225 pieces, wooden.

King George VI and Princesses Elizabeth and Margaret on horseback. Chad Valley, 105 pieces, wooden, c.1939.

Coronation Procession, 1937. Waddington, 470 pieces, cardboard.

Portrait of Edward VIII. Mammoth, over 400 pieces, cardboard, 1936. Chad Valley and Victory did similar portraits.

Far left: Jubilee portrait of the King and Queen, 1935. Lumar, 270 pieces, cardboard.

Left: Princess Elizabeth and Princess Margaret Rose, from a Marcus Adams photograph. Chad Valley, 225 pieces, wooden, c.1937.

ROYAL PUZZLES

Trooping the Colour. A.V.N. Jones, 150 pieces, wooden, c.1938.

The Queen and Prince Charles. Chad Valley, 108 pieces, wooden, c.1952.

The Queen and Prince Philip's Silver Jubilee. Maker unknown, 500 pieces, cardboard, 1977. Note the photographer in the mirror.

Queen Elizabeth the Queen Mother, Royal Jig-Saw No.1. Philmar, 500 pieces, cardboard, c.1980.

BRITISH JIGSAW PUZZLE CLUB

Illuminations. Superb puzzle depicting religious scenes, 626 pieces, wooden, c.1950.

PUZZLE CLUBS

Gathering Flowers. Miss K.M. Briscoe, Eastbourne, 228 pieces, c.1930.

Madonna and Child. The Original Jigsaw Puzzle Club, London, 450 pieces, wooden, c.1930.

The Skier, probably from a poster. The British Jigsaw Puzzle Club, 516 pieces, wooden, c.1930.

Miss Rutherford in her studio, 1950.

The Blue Dress. Miss Rutherford's Puzzle Club, Liverpool, 350 pieces, wooden, c.1950.

PEARS

Naughty Boy or *Compulsory Education* by Briton Riviere. 600 pieces, wooden, 1909.

EARLY WOODEN PUZZLES

Bathing Beauties. A.1. Puzzle Club, 1000 pieces, wooden, c.1920.

The Toyshop. Victory Supercut, period interior, 800 pieces, c.1920.

SPORTING WOODEN PUZZLES

The Harefield Harriers by Cecil Aldin. The British Jigsaw Club, 730 pieces, wooden, c.1935.

Christmas in Canada. Maker unknown, 400 pieces, wooden, c.1910.

Winter in Amsterdam. The Graphic Jigsaw Puzzle, 264 pieces, wooden, c.1910.

FIELD SPORTS

Lady with Guns and Game. Maker unknown, 300 pieces, wooden, c.1930.

Gone to Ground. Fox hunting scene from Redland Lending Library, Bristol. Chad Valley, 300 pieces, wooden, c.1938.

RAPHAEL TUCK WOODEN PUZZLES

William Shakespeare reading 'Loves Labours Lost' to Queen Elizabeth and her court. 100 pieces, c.1920.

Lady In Pink. Zag-Zaw, 150 pieces, c.1910.

Boys with their Tops. Period study, 150 pieces, c.1905.

RAPHAEL TUCK ZAG-ZAW WOODEN PUZZLES

Top: *Among the Gorse* by I.D. Graham. 350 pieces, wooden, 1925.

Above, left to right: *Take this back to Tipperary*. 250 pieces, wooden, c.1918; *The Pickwick Papers*. 165 pieces, wooden, 1912.

Left: *Trooping the Colour. No.3 The King and Royal Princes arriving at Horse Guard's Parade*. 150 pieces, wooden, c.1930.

RAPHAEL TUCK WOODEN PUZZLES

Election at Eatonswill. The hustings in a cartoon-type puzzle, 400 pieces, c.1910.

The Wagon Train. Later puzzle, with whimsies, 650 pieces, c.1930.

DELTA WOODEN PUZZLES

Golfe de la Gotat Res Toulon. 280 pieces, c.1925.

The Pantiles, Tunbridge Wells. 520 pieces, wooden, c.1930.

Queen Elizabeth with Sir Walter Raleigh. 600 pieces, c.1925.

Prince Rupert. 290 pieces, c.1925.

CHAD VALLEY FOR GREAT WESTERN RAILWAY

Caerphilly Castle. First G.W.R. puzzle sold at Empire Exhibition in 1924, 150 non-interlocking pieces, wooden. Rare box.

St. Julian. G.W.R. steamer to Channel Islands, 150 pieces, wooden, 1926-28.

Royal Route to the West. 150-200 pieces, wooden. 'Cornish Riviera' hauled by King Class Loco *George V.* From *Illustrated London News,* c.1933-39.

CHAD VALLEY FOR GREAT WESTERN RAILWAY

King Arthur on Dartmoor. Impressive mythical scene, 375-400 pieces, wooden, 1931-36.

Drake goes West. Dated 1572, Plymouth scene, 400 pieces, with descriptive leaflet, wooden, 1934-39.

CHAD VALLEY FOR GREAT WESTERN RAILWAY

Locomotives Old and New. Compares Lord of the Isles and King George V locomotives, 150-200 pieces, wooden, 1934-39.

Cornish Riviera Express. Abbotsbury Castle Loco with train at Dawlish, 150-200 pieces, wooden, c.1927-36.

The Night Mail. 200 pieces, wooden, 1934-36.

CHAD VALLEY FOR GREAT WESTERN RAILWAY

G.W. Locos in the Making. School party looking around the Swindon Works, 150-200 pieces, wooden, 1936-39.

Windsor Castle. Stylized view across the Thames to the castle, oval-shaped, 150 pieces, wooden, 1926-30.

Model Railway. Period picture from 1930s, 150-200 pieces, wooden, 1934-39.

Britain's Mightiest, King George V. Stylized picture of King Class Loco, 150 pieces, wooden, 1927-30.

Streamlined Way. New diesel railway car with 'ghost' of King George V behind, 150-200 pieces, wooden, 1934-38.

London Highways. Promoting Carter Patterson, G.W. Road Haulage Co. Shows London Bridge, 150-200 pieces, wooden, 1934-36.

CHAD VALLEY FOR GREAT WESTERN RAILWAY

From left to right. Top: *Romans at Caerleon*. 150-200 pieces, wooden, 1933-39; *The Fishguard Army, 1797*. 150-200 pieces, wooden, 1934-39.

Middle: *Windsor Castle* (with knights). 150-200 pieces, wooden, 1931-33; *Historic Totnes*. 150-300 pieces, wooden, 1933-39.

Bottom: *Cornish Fishing Village*. 150 pieces, wooden, 1930-33; *Piccadilly Circus*. 200 pieces, wooden, 1933-37.

CHAD VALLEY WOODEN PUZZLES, POST-WAR LINERS

R.M.S. *Queen Elizabeth*.
120 pieces, c.1946.

SS Caronia. View of deck, 70
pieces, c.1946.

SS Saxonia. Cunard
liner, 200 pieces, with
unusual box, c.1947.

CHAD VALLEY PROMOTIONAL PUZZLES

O.H.M.S. Army.

To the Highest Standard.

Above and left: Four of
the Dunlop Series of
twelve 200-piece puzzles,
wooden, c.1935.

Yorkminster

Westminster.

Imperial and International Communications. World map with
leaflet, 150 pieces, c.1932.

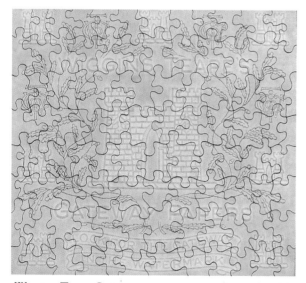

Wiggins Teape *Gateway* paper watermarks puzzle with
booklet, 100 pieces, c.1935.

The Hoover Factory at Perivale Middlesex. 200 pieces, c.1936.

MIXED UP AND UNUSUAL PUZZLES

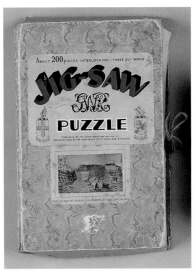

Van Riebeeck landing at Cape of Good Hope. Chad Valley for G.W. R. box, but A.V.N. Jones cut, 200 pieces, c.1946.

Box for G.W.R. mixed-up puzzle on left.

King George V 1927-36. Chad Valley for G.W.R., 150-200 pieces, but two halves of puzzle do not match as a picture, evidence of stack-cutting and questionable quality control, c.1930.

Caterpillar Tractor. Cuneo painting, cut with fretsaw by Oliver Tyler, amateur, 40 pieces, c.1944.

Camera Girl. Maker unknown, 160 pieces, wooden, c.1925.

PRE-WAR SHIP PUZZLES

M.V. Britannic. Intalok White Star liner, 150 pieces, wooden, c.1933. (White Star and Cunard merged in 1934.)

SS *Caernarvon Castle*, Union Castle liner. A.V.N. Jones, Transport Series, 150 pieces, wooden, c.1938.

Huskisson Dock, Liverpool. Chad Valley for Cunard, 150 pieces, wooden, 1926-33.

SS *Matiana* and another B.I. ship. Chad Valley for British India, 150 pieces, wooden, c.1930.

Seafront at New York (R.M.S. Aquitania). Chad Valley for Cunard, 150 pieces, wooden, 1926-33.

SS *Nevasa in Kiel Canal.* Chad Valley for British India Steam Navigation Co. Ltd. 150-200 pieces, wooden, c.1935.

R.M.S. Queen Mary

Artist's impression issued before the ship was named and launched. Chad Valley for Cunard, 150-200-400 pieces, wooden, c.1933-50.

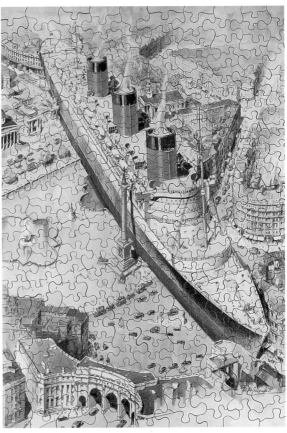

Queen Mary in Trafalgar Square. Chad Valley for Cunard, 150-300 pieces, wooden, c.1936.

Maker unknown, improved photograph, 250 pieces, wooden, c.1938.

Victory, artist's impression, 350 pieces, wooden, c.1935.

Salmon Academy, 250 pieces, wooden, c.1935.

WARTIME PUZZLES

The A.T.S. and their vehicles. Waddington, 135 pieces, cardboard, c.1944.

Friend or Foe? Victory, 240 pieces, wooden, c.1917.

The Fleet at Gibraltar. Chad Valley for Arthur Balfour & Sons, 400 pieces, wooden, c.1938.

R.A.F. Spitfire Fighter Plane. Compojig, 220 pieces, thick card, c.1945.

R.A.F. planes - the build up to the Second World War. Over 400 pieces, cardboard, c.1938.

AIRCRAFT PUZZLES

Above: *De Haviland Hercules Airliner over the Pyramids.*
Salmon Academy, 100 pieces, wooden, c.1936.
Left: *Helicopters (no.540).* Waddington (Air B.P.)
circular, 500 pieces, cardboard, c.1960.

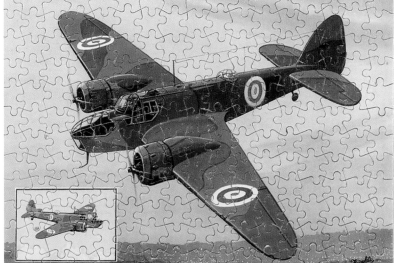

Hawker Hart. Victory, 60 pieces, wooden, c.1937.

Blenheim Bomber. Fairylite, 225 pieces, cardboard, c.1950.

Above: *Space Station.* Victory (Spears), 125
pieces, wooden, c.1970.
Left: Hurricane shooting down German
bomber. Maker unknown, 250 pieces,
cardboard, c.1945.

FLYING THE FLAG

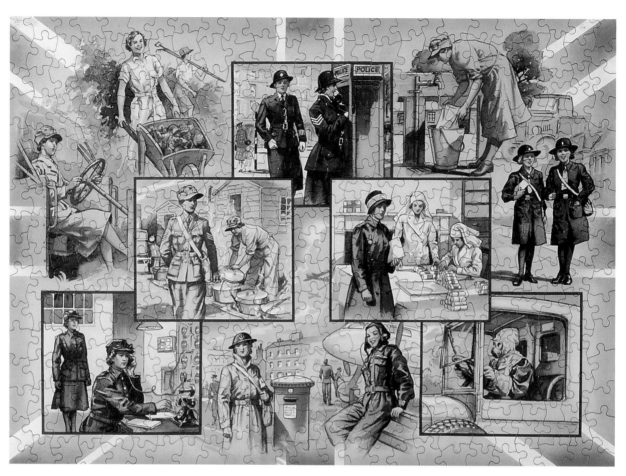

Men of Britain and *Women of Britain* puzzles of the Wartime Auxilliary Services. Waddington, 400 pieces, cardboard, c.1941.

PUZZLE BOXES, 1900-1939

Boxes include: Peacock *King and Court*, Zig-Zag, Chloe Preston, Glevum, Peacock Map, *Pip, Squeak and Wilfred*, *Tuck Tippe Toppe*, *Bonzo*, Hamleys, Photocrom, Delta, Victory, Schoolbred *Elves*, and the Zig-Zag *Hands Only*.

CHILDREN'S DESIGNER PUZZLES

The Pied Piper. En-Thrall-Us, 50 pieces, wooden, c.1930.

Little Red Riding Hood. W.G. Evans, 75 pieces, wooden, c.1910.

The Young Sportsman. Chloe Preston Series, A.V.N. Jones, 75 pieces, wooden, c.1925.

Lost. Maker unknown, 140 pieces, wooden, c.1923.

Above: Mabel Lucie Attwell. Maker unknown, 50 pieces, cardboard, c.1935.
Right: *The Shadow on the Wall.* Bonzo Series by G. Studdy, A.V.N. Jones, 110 pieces, wooden, c.1925.

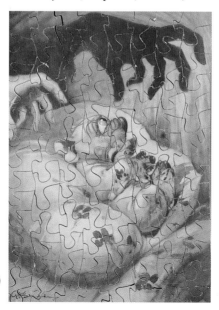

Mickey Mouse. Chad Valley, 120 pieces, wooden, c.1925.

SHAW'S 'MATCHLESS SERIES', CARDBOARD, 120-PIECE

1147 Formation Flying, c.1935.

1107 Changing the Guard, c.1935.

1119 Trooping the Colours, c.1935.

1118 Tally Ho, c.1935.

1120 Mauritania, c.1935.

1116 Peter Pan, c.1935.

Mammoth Cardboard Puzzles, Over 400 Pieces, 1930s

London Pool (no.38).

Step On It (no.6). Brooklands race track.

Norfolk Broads (no.35).

D.H. Comet (no.22). Recording a notable flight.

Neck and Neck (no.1).

British Ambulances (no.77).

LUMAR PUZZLES, CARDBOARD, 1930S

R.M.S. Queen Elizabeth, 230 pieces.

Hunting Story, 250 pieces.

English Village, 250 pieces.

Houses of Parliament, 260 pieces.

Panda (no.2), 260 pieces.

Harvesting, 260 pieces.

Lambeth Walk, signed jigsaw puzzle, 250 pieces.

Sectional views of R.M.S. Aquitania, 1926-39, 30(

BY CHAD VALLEY

... TO TOPS OF FUNNELS 164 FEET—HEIGHT TO MASTHEADS 220 FEET—ACCOMMODATION FOR NEARLY 5,000.

...en; and *R.M.S. Queen Mary*, c.1939, 500 pieces, wooden.

EARLY WOODEN PUZZLES FROM MINOR COMPANIES

Floral Glories. Upton Tower Jigsaw, 400 pieces, wooden, c.1930.

The Gate to the Mosque. The Kwiz, 300 pieces, wooden, 1925.

Speed. Valentine, 150 pieces, wooden, c.1936.

St. Ives, Cornwall by Terence McCaw. Fortnum and Mason, 150 pieces, wooden, c.1930.

ARTISTS' PUZZLES

Country Dance by William Heath Robinson. An exceptional cutting, 500 pieces, wooden, c.1930.

Good Morning from a photograph by Carbonetti. Bon Marche, London, 260 pieces, wooden, c.1910.

Unhappy and Curly after Louis Wain. Maker unknown, 100 pieces, wooden, 1910.

EARLY CARDBOARD PUZZLES

Gallant Encounter. Tru-Cut, Regency scene, 260 pieces, c.1960.

Prisoner of Zenda. Waddington, scene from the David Selznick film production, 439 pieces, c.1938.

Sleepy Lane (no.1). Tower Press, Select Series, painting by Leonard Squirrel, 400 pieces, c.1955.

Down by the Sea. Tower Press, Good Companions Series, post-war optimism, 400 pieces, c.1948.

Development of Trains. Tower Press, popular wartime puzzle cut in half, 400 pieces, cardboard, c.1943.

Queen Elizabeth Visits her Ships (no.109). Waddington, popular historical scene, 470 pieces, c.1950.

COMPETITION AND DETECTIVE PUZZLES

Inspector Hornleigh Investigates - Forced Landing. Waddington, 200 pieces, cardboard. Do the puzzle to solve the murder, the solution is written in invisible ink, c.1938.

Killer on Board. Waddington Cluedo Jig-Saw, 750 pieces, cardboard, 1996.

Left: *Popular Dogs* with £5000 in prizes; right: *Find the Films,* giant jig-saw with £3000 in prizes; Daily Mail, each over 400 pieces, cardboard. There was also a *Film Stars* puzzle, 1930s.

Left: *Name the Village,* mystery puzzle. Mammoth, over 400 pieces, cardboard, 1935. Where is this village? We offer a prize to any reader who can identify it by sending a photograph of the same scene today.

Right: Box for Mammoth puzzle.

JIGSAW PUZZLE GAMES

Jig-A-Lotto. Popular pre-war game, four 35-piece puzzles, published by John Knight Ltd., Soap Makers, as a promotional advertisement, cardboard, c.1935.

Progressive Game. Chad Valley, six puzzles for races at parties, 80 pieces, wooden, c.1936.

EARLY WADDINGTON CARDBOARD CIRCULAR PUZZLES

Evolution of the Merchant Ship (no.206). 383 pieces, c.1946.

Travel Through the Ages (no.202). 500 pieces, c.1938.

London Views (no.204). 500 pieces, c.1942.

A.R.P. Design (no.203). World War II puzzle, 381 pieces, c.1941.

CAR PUZZLES

Ride in a Coach. A.V.N. Jones, 100 pieces, wooden, c.1932.

Development of the Motor Car. Tower Press, cut in half, 400 pieces, cardboard, c.1940.

Truimph Herald. Victory Popular Series, 150 pieces, wooden, c.1965.

Father's Workshop by Tony Smith. Waddington, 350 pieces, cardboard, 1995.

Filling up at the Blacksmith. Gibson's Games, 1000 pieces, cardboard, 1997.

VICTORY CLASSIC WOODEN PUZZLES

Four of the *Cathedral* series of 125-piece puzzles: *Winchester, Canterbury, Exeter, Worcester.*

The Market Place. Line drawing with overpainting of medieval market scene, 1000 pieces, c.1930.

VICTORY PUZZLES

Caught Napping. Artistic Puzzles, 300 pieces, c.1958.

Fruit and Flowers. Artistic Puzzles, 400 pieces, c.1955.

The Brownies. 100 pieces, wooden, c.1960.

Dagenham Girl Pipers. 175 pieces, wooden, c.1946.

The Queen of Hearts. Nursery Rhyme Series, 80 pieces, wooden, 1960.

The Dog Jigsaw Puzzle (including 12 cut-out dogs). 75 pieces, wooden, c.1935.

EARLY VICTORY AND CHAD VALLEY PUZZLES

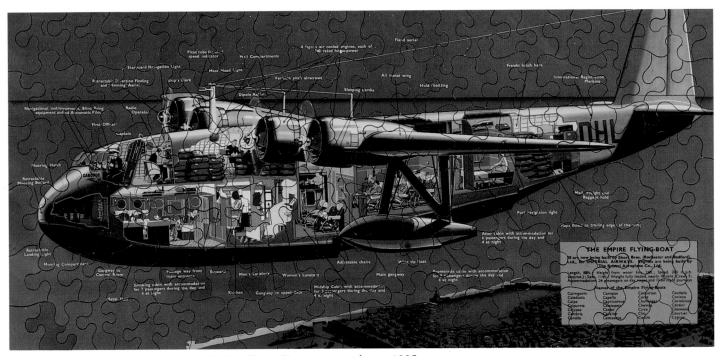

Imperial Airways Empire Flying Boat. Chad Valley, 150 pieces, wooden, c.1935.

Hengist Airliner. Victory, 200 pieces, wooden, c.1935.

Romney Hythe and Dymchurch Railway Locomotive. Victory Constructional Puzzles, 3-D effect, 150 pieces, wooden, c.1960.

Centre right: *SS United States* and above, *Union Castle Liner.* Victory Constructional Puzzles, 3-D effect, 150 pieces, wooden, c.1960.

SAILING SHIPS

Herzogen Cecile from the painting by R. Back. Wentworth, laser-cut 250 pieces, wooden, 1997.

H.M.S. Victory, (no.J714). Salmon Academy, 100 pieces, wooden, c.1930.

Trafalgar. The British Jigsaw Puzzle Club, 180 pieces, wooden, c.1930.

Race for Harbour. Mammoth, over 400 pieces, cardboard, c.1935.

PROMOTIONAL PUZZLES

The South Bank Exhibition, Festival of Britain 1951. Efroc, 125 pieces, wooden.

Gidea Park Estate, Essex. Town and Country Homes, 100 pieces, wooden, c.1930.

Advertisement for Cobra Floor Polish. Blyth & Platt Co. Ltd., 160 pieces, cardboard, c.1940.

Centennial Exhibition, New Zealand, Wonders of the World No.12. William Ellis & Co. Ltd., 200 pieces, cardboard, 1940.

The Princesses visit Ming the Panda, Wonders of the World No.9. William Ellis & Co. Ltd., 200 pieces, cardboard, c.1938.

MAP PUZZLES

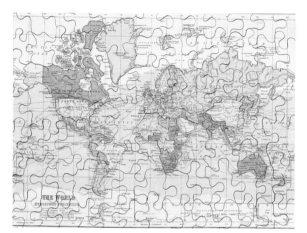

Above: *The World*. Victory, 90 pieces, wooden, 1930s.
Right: *Industrial Europe*. Victory, 130 pieces, wooden, 1930s.

Industrial Life in England. Victory
educational puzzle, about 100 pieces,
wooden, c.1965.

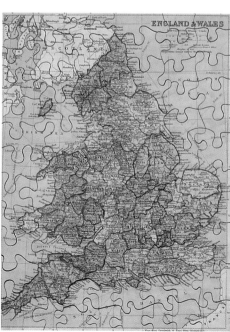

Above and right: *Map of England
and Scotland*. Veltoy, 70 pieces,
wooden, c.1955.

Map of England. William Peacock's popular Map
Puzzles, 220 pieces, wooden, c.1900.

DISNEY WELCOM PUZZLES BY WILLIAM ELLIS & CO. LTD.

Mickey's Donkey. Over 200 pieces, c.1950.

Mickey's Fire Engine. Over 200 pieces, c.1950

Goofy's Trailer. Over 200 pieces, c.1950.

Stealing the Giant's Supper. Over 200 pieces, c.1950.

Brave Little Tailor. Over 200 pieces, cardboard, c.1940.

Ferdinand the Bull. Over 200 pieces, cardboard, 1940.

PAGES FROM CATALOGUES

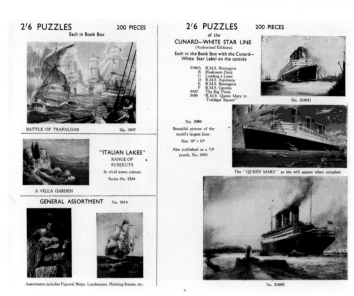

Chad Valley, 1935.

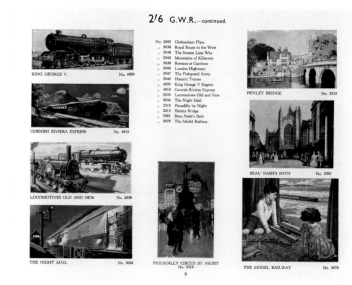

Chad Valley, 1935.

Chad Valley, 1935.

Waddington, c.1938.

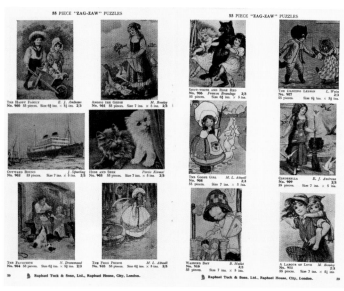

Raphael Tuck, c.1930.

Raphael Tuck, c.1930.

MINIATURE PUZZLES

Four postcard puzzles in aid of John Millard Memorial Women's Guild, 40 pieces, cardboard, c.1935.

Bubbles. Pears' postcard, 35 pieces, cardboard, c.1938.

Map of the British Isles, 24 pieces, wooden, c.1990.

Two promotional puzzles. Gee Graphics, cut by water jet, 165 pieces, wooden, 1996.

Photograph cut into family puzzle, 12 pieces, wooden, 1995.

Local Views, Exeter Cathedral. Salmon Academy, 36 pieces, wooden, c.1930.

Most miniature puzzle pieces requiring magnifying glass and tweezers. Cut by water-jet, 80 pieces, wooden, c.1995

Kings College Chapel, Cambridge, wooden, 25 pieces, c.1935.

CHILDREN'S PUZZLES

Above: *Little Foal*, Victory, 60 pieces, c.1930.
Left: *The Children's Box of Trains Dissected Puzzles*. Maker unknown, 20 pieces, wooden, c.1912.

The Treasure Ship. Victory, 175 pieces, c.1938

Tom, Tom the Piper's Son. Victory, 104 pieces, c.1934

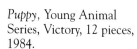

Steam Roller. Traction Engine Series, Victory, 80 pieces, c.1965.

Indians. Victory, 55 shaped pieces, c.1960.

Above from the top: *Road Roller*, Philip & Tracey, 25 pieces, cardboard, c.1970.

Guardsmen, Good Wood Playthings, 10 pieces, c.1965.

Puppy, Young Animal Series, Victory, 12 pieces, 1984.

St. Paul's Cathedral. Victory, 100 pieces, c.1965.

Seaside Traffic. Victory, 60 pieces, c.1970

The Fire Engine. George Luck, 37 pieces, wooden, c.1990.

TOWER PRESS 'GOOD COMPANIONS SERIES', CARDBOARD

River Boat Skiffle (no.78). 400 pieces, 1960s.

The Sawdust Ring (no.30). 400 pieces, 1960s.

Comets over Africa (no.29). 400 pieces, 1960s.

In the Paddock (no.54). 400 pieces, 1960s.

Arc de Triomphe (no.14). 400 pieces, 1960s.

Television Studio (no.60). 400 pieces, 1960s.

RAILWAY PUZZLES, CARDBOARD

B.1. at York. Age of Steam no.2. Arrow Games, 500 pieces, c.1970.

Cornish Riviera At Dawlish. Age of Steam no.2. Arrow Games, 500 pieces, c.1965.

Royal Scot. Age of Steam no.3. Arrow Games, 500 pieces, c.1965.

School's Class, Southern, (Stowe). Falcon Games, 300 pieces, c.1975.

Mallard, L.N.E.R. Falcon Games, 300 pieces, c.1975.

Locomotion. Tower Press, scene on Keighley & Worth Valley Railway, 500 pieces, c.1970.

3-D PUZZLES

Bildajig no.1 Cargo Liner, length 11ins; no.2 Passenger Liner, length 16ins, c.1930. *Bildajig Ships*, Scottish Toys, tug, c.1930.

"BILDAJIG"
PATENT NO. 419311

"BILDAJIG" No. 2B (Black Hull).
(Trade Mark.) No. 2W (White Hull).

Appl. for Patent No. 14124.

Model of "Passenger Liner"--16 in. long.

A CONSTRUCTIONAL game of absorbing interest which, in this particular number, calls for the solving of a series of Jig-Saw Puzzles, in which the Model of a **"Passenger Liner"** is built up Deck by Deck by layer construction.

There are 6 Decks—from the Boat Deck "A" to "B," "C," "D," "E" and "F"—also Funnel Casing, Bridge Pieces, etc.

Start with the base, and on this proceed to build upwards. Each Deck is different, showing Cabins, Saloons, Lounges, etc., and each Deck is really a separate puzzle.

As you go along you will find it useful to peg in a Ventilator, Mast or Funnel where you think it belongs, removing and replacing same as you add another Deck.

Edge Colour and Shape also provide guidance.

FINALLY—Funnels, Masts and Ventilators all in their proper locations and pressed well in will, with the inter-locking construction, hold the completed Model in position.

The ten small Ship's Boats may now be gently pressed into their positions as marked on the Boat Deck.

You will enjoy solving this entrancing Puzzle and you will like the Model when finished.

No. 0 makes a "Tug-Boat," 7 in. long. No. 1 makes a "Cargo Liner," 11 in. long.

"BILDAJIG" (TRADE MARK.) **Nos. 2B and 2W.**

MADE BY SCOTTISH TOYS LTD. GLASGOW.

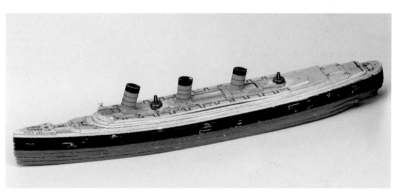

R.M.S. *Queen Mary*. Chad Valley 'take to pieces' model, twelve removable decks, separate masts, 12 pieces, c.1936.

Globe - The World's Only Spherical Jigsaw Puzzle. B.V. Leisure, 500 pieces, c.1995.

The Globe, Sculpture Puzzles. Really Useful Games, 170 pieces, 1997.

'GILES' PUZZLES, CARDBOARD

Three 300-piece puzzles published by Beaverbrook Newspapers from the covers of *Giles* annuals. *Mad Hatter's Tea Party* (1957), *The Fruit Shop* (1972), and *The Giant Snowball* (1973), c.1975.

LATER WADDINGTON CARDBOARD CIRCULAR PUZZLES

Sporting Dogs (no.577B). 500 pieces, c.1980.

Tokyo Olympics 1964 (no.545). 500 pieces.

Four Seasons (no.05941). 500 pieces, c.1985.

British Waders (no.516). 500 pieces, c.1980.

R.M.S. TITANIC

Falcon Games produced these twin 500-piece cardboard puzzles showing the famous liner, c.1992.

DISNEY AND OTHER CHILDREN'S CARTOON PUZZLES

Far Tottering Branch Line by Roland Emett. Maker unknown, classic Emett cartoon railway, 120 pieces, cardboard, c1960.

Disneyfantasyland. Waddington, 30 pieces, cardboard, c.1970.

The Lion King. Ravensburger, Walt Disney, three 49-piece puzzles with scenes from the film, cardboard, 1997.

Snow White and the Seven Dwarfs. Waddington, Walt Disney, 500 pieces, cardboard, 1996.

Walt Disney Feature Film (101 Dalmations). Ravensburger, 200 pieces, cardboard, 1997.

PUZZLING PUZZLES

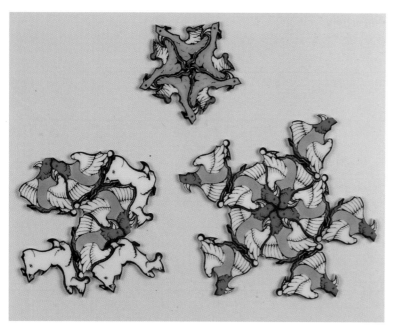

Perplexing Poultry. Pentaplex by Sir Roger Penrose, 200 pieces, plastic, 1990.

British Isles Animal Map. George Luck, 47 pieces, wooden, 1997.

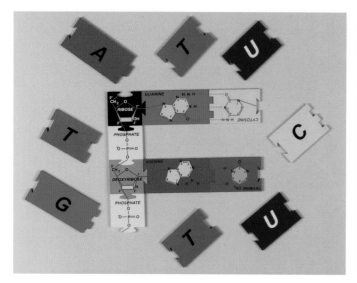

Above left: *D.N.A. Chain Puzzle.* Gee Graphics, 8 pieces, plastic, 1997

Above right: *Executive C.E. Scroll,* Tomahawk Toys, 24 pieces, wooden, 1997.

Left: *Black Panther,* cut by Tom Tyler, 220 pieces (some interchangeable), wooden, 1997.

FANTASY, REPRODUCTION AND DELICIOUS PUZZLES

Top left: *Piccadilly Circus, 1950*, and middle left: *The Lure of the Underground*. Cheatwell Games, Art on the Tube Series (reproduced by permission of the London Transport Museum), 1000 pieces, cardboard 1997.

Top right: *Treebeard* by Rodney Matthews. Falcon Games, 625 pieces, cardboard, 1997.

Middle right: *Lost in Transit*. Chad Valley G.W.R., 144 pieces, wooden, 1938. Feenix reproduction c.1993.

Mary Berry Recipe Jigsaw. Bear, Bear & Bear, 500 pieces, cardboard, 1997.

WADDINGTON '3-D PUZZ'

The Millennium Falcon, 857 foam pieces, 1997.

The Capitol Building, Washington, 718 foam pieces, 1996.

CONSERVATION AND WILDLIFE PUZZLES

Sun, Sand, Sea and Sky. James Hamilton, 1000 pieces, cardboard, 1994.

Butterfly Garden. Michael Stanfield circular puzzle, designed by Julie Piper for Royal Society for Nature Conservation, 300 pieces, cardboard, c.1985.

Rainforest Parrots. James Hamilton, 1000 pieces, cardboard, 1997.

Tawny Owl by David Binns. Waddington, for the Royal Society for the Protection of Birds, 90 pieces, cardboard, c.1970.

The Pond. Orchard Toys, 202 pieces, cardboard, 1997.

The Seasons. Falcon Games, one of four circular 200-piece cardboard puzzles depicting *Autumn, Winter, Spring* and *Summer,* 1997.

GIBSON GAMES, 1000-PIECE, CARDBOARD

Little Gems, c.1996.

Eminent Victorians. History of Victorian transport progress, c.1996.

The House of Lords. Interior View Series, c.1996.

The Bar Car, Orient Express, c.1996.

MANDOLIN PUZZLES

Noble Game of Cricket. One hundred of the game's outstanding players. 1000 pieces, cardboard, 1997.

Second World War. The history of the conflict. 1000 pieces, cardboard, 1997.

COTTAGE, GARDEN AND ALPINE SCENES

Cottage, Hampshire. Waddington, 1000 pieces, cardboard, c.1996.

Reflections on an Alpine Lake. Falcon Games, 500 pieces, cardboard, 1997.

Kemerton Cottage, Hereford and Worcestershire. Falcon Games, Country Cottages Series, 1000 pieces, cardboard, c.1997.

Alpine View. Falcon Games, Harmony Series, 1000 pieces, cardboard, 1997.

Vico Morcote (Canton Ticino) with Monte Generoso. Squire amateur cut, about 500 pieces, wooden, c.1968.

Packwood House and Gardens, Lapworth, Hants. Falcon Games, Gardens Series, 500 pieces, cardboard, c.1996.

MODERN CHILDREN'S PUZZLES

English Woodland. Robert Longstaff, laser-cut floor puzzle, 48 large pieces, wooden, 1996.

South American Jungle. Robert Longstaff, laser-cut floor puzzle, 24 large pieces, wooden, 1996.

Thomas the Tank Engine. Ravensburger, 40 pieces, cardboard, 1997.

Concorde. Paul and Marjorie Abbatt Toys Ltd., 48 pieces, wooden, 1970.

A *Close Shave*. Ravensburger, Wallace and Gromit, 500 pieces, cardboard, 1997.

HANDLEY PRINTERS 'J.R. PUZZLES'
500-PIECE, CARDBOARD, C.1997

Top: *The Road Menders*, showing road roller; above: *In Days of Steam* showing traction engine etc. Halcyon Days Series.

Top: *Lakeland, Ashness Bridge*, a typical Lake District scene; above: *Welford on Avon* with thatched cottages.

Reflections, a dazzling Autumn scene.

Edwardian Collection, a London street scene from an old photograph.

COLLECTORS' PUZZLES

Trumps General Store.
Waddington, 150
household items
masquerading as General
Store objects, 1000
pieces, cardboard, 1997.

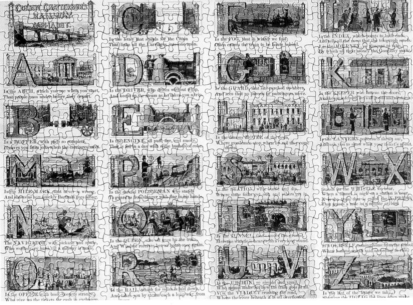

Railway Alphabet.
Cranham Publications,
500 pieces, cardboard,
1997.

Stamps of the World.
Cranham Publications,
500 pieces, cardboard,
1997.

RAVENSBURGER

Tutankhamun. 1000 pieces, cardboard, 1997.

Rain Forest. 1500 pieces, cardboard, 1997.

The Ballet Class by Degas. 1500 pieces, cardboard, 1997.

In Space. 200 pieces, glows in the dark, cardboard, 1997.

OUT OF DOORS

Winter Wayfarers by B.J. Freeman. Waddington, 500 pieces, c.1992.

Picnic by Don Breckon. Waddington, G.W.R. scene, 500 pieces, 1990.

Gay Interlude. Philmar, 900 pieces, cardboard, c.1970.

George V. G.W.R. King Class Loco. Hope, 500 pieces, cardboard, c.1975.

Windsor Castle. Gibson Games, Aerial View Series, 1000 pieces, cardboard, 1995.

I Love London. Michael Jupp Collection, Waddington, 1000 pieces, cardboard, c.1996.

LASER-CUT WOODEN PUZZLES

Above: *Last British Rail Steam-Hauled Train.* Wentworth, 250 pieces, 1996.

Left: *Stone Wall.* Wentworth, 425 pieces, 1995.

Below: *Worcester Cathedral.* Waddington, 500 pieces, c.1989.

CURRENT WOODEN PUZZLES

Dante and Beatrice. Meredith Worsfold,
750 pieces, wooden, c.1990.

Dolphins. Robert Longstaff Workshops, laser-cut 864 pieces, wooden, 1997.

Water Lily Pond by Monet. Optimago, 441
pieces, wooden, 1992.

HAND-CUT PUZZLES

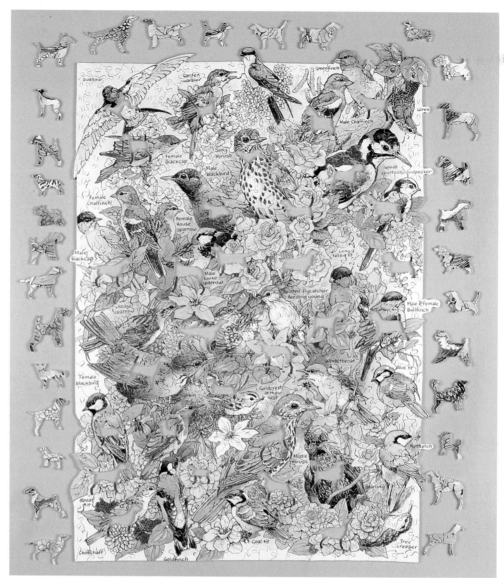

Garden Birds. Sara White, with thirty-four different British dogs cut as whimsies, 1050 pieces, wooden, 1996.

Sailing Ship. Puzzleplex, Peter Stocken, 250 pieces, wooden, c.1990.

CHAPTER 9

TWENTIETH CENTURY BRITISH JIGSAW PUZZLE MANUFACTURERS

In attempting to list this century's manufacturers one inevitably finds significant differences in the amount of material available. The larger and longest producing companies have easily accessible histories and some of those still in business can be visited in order to see their work and techniques at first-hand. In the case of many of the older manufacturers, however, little remains but the maker's name on a tattered box of an old wooden or cardboard jigsaw puzzle. Some did not even put their names to their product nor a date or place of manufacture though most proudly declared that they were 'British Made'.

The problem is compounded by the fact that in the first three decades of the century it was extremely easy to set up in business as a maker of wooden jigsaw puzzles. There were probably hundreds if not thousands of such makers, many of whom stayed in production for a year or two. It was a good way of tiding oneself over a period of unemployment in the 1920s and 1930s.

I have listed the companies alphabetically and have also listed the names of specific series of puzzles, referencing them to their manufacturer as in some cases the name of the series, rather than the manufacturer, appears on the box. The list which follows is unavoidably incomplete and I hope that readers will, over the course of time, add to it.

A.1. Puzzle Club, London. c.1920-1939. Wide variety of hand-cut wooden jigsaws in distinctive brown, cube-shaped boxes.

Adydos Ltd., Thorne Estate, North Eastern Road, Thorne, Doncaster, S. Yorks, DN3 4AS. No longer in production. Cardboard. *Heritage Series* for National Trust etc.

Academy Series, see Salmon.

Allen Ltd., Ian, Coombelands House, Coombelands Lane, Addlestone, Surrey, KT15 IHY. c.1950-c.1970 Publisher of books, especially railway subjects. Wooden and cardboard. Mainly railway subjects.

Archers Jigsaws, see Handley Printers.

Armitage Bros. Ltd., Nottingham. 1950s? Thin cardboard. One puzzle only? Advertising puzzle for Armitages Chick Food.

Army and Navy Co-operative Society Ltd., 105, Victoria Street, London SW1. c.1930s. Wooden mosaic puzzle.

Arrow Games, 14 West Road, Tottenham, London N17 ORF. No longer in production. See Chap. 5.

Arty-Zan, Fairholme Farm, 14 Croydon Lane, Banstead, Surrey, SM7 3AN. 1990. Produces personalised cardboard jigsaw puzzles in four sizes, from customers' pictures.

Ashley Puzzles produced by Arrow, see above.

Associated Newspapers Ltd., London. c.1960s. Two cardboard puzzles in a model cut-out book. Probably made elsewhere and a one-off.

Austin, Ann, 19, Beauchamp Place, Brompton Road, London. 1936. Probably very limited production. Wooden.

Austin Project Marketing Ltd. c.1975. No longer producing puzzles. Cardboard. *Delecto Series.*

Bacon & Co., G.W. 127 Strand, London. 1930s. No longer in production. Wooden. *Bacon's Reversible.*

Baker & Co., John, 6 Kensington High Street, London. 1910. No longer in production. Wooden. *Perplexing Jigsaw Puzzles.*

Bear, Bear & Bear Ltd., Greatham, Rutland, LE15 7NG. c.1990. Cardboard. *Mary Berry Recipe Jigsaw.*

Beaux Arts, Great Britain. 1930s. No longer in production. Wooden .

Beaverbrook Newspapers, Fleet Street, London. c.1974. Cardboard. Three *Giles* cartoons from covers of annuals. One-off.

Bedford, England. c.1930s. Wooden. Series name for puzzles produced by F. Warne & Co.

Belinda, Golden Gate Products. c.1960. Cardboard.

Bellow & Higden, see Palitoy Co.

Bentalls Store Ltd., Kingston-on-Thames, Surrey. c.1955. Probably very limited production. Thin plywood. *Tip Top* picture puzzle.

Beraton, 89 Church Road, Hove, East Sussex. 1930s. No longer in production. Wooden. Traditional English scenes. Considerable output.

Berry, Mary, see Bear, Bear & Bear Ltd.

Beryl Series, made by C. & Co.

Beverley. Tower Press Series.

Big Top Puzzle, England. c.1970s. No longer in production. Cardboard? Manufactured by another company.

Big Value Jigsaw Puzzle, England. c.1930s. No longer in production. Wooden.

Big Jigs, Elham, Canterbury. 1990s. Wooden and cardboard.

Bildajig, Glasgow, Scotland. 1930s. No longer in production. Wooden. Unusual 3-D ship puzzles. Only three types known, two liners and a tug.

Bon Marche, Brixton, London. 1910. No longer in production. Wooden. *Gems from the Art Galleries.* Probably very limited production.

Bond, E.E. 7 White Lodge, Parkstone Road, Poole, Dorset, England. 1969. No longer in production. Wooden. Very limited production.

Boots The Chemist. 1930s. Wooden. Made for them by Chad Valley and others. Special leaflet produced.

British Beauty Spots. 1930s. Wooden. Probably a series produced by another manufacturer.

British Isles Jigsaw Map. c.1960s. Cardboard. No identified maker.

British Legion Poppy Factory, Richmond, Surrey. c.1950s. Limited production. Wooden.

Bulmer's Cider Co. Ltd., Hereford. 1970. Cardboard. One-off of their preserved King George V engine.

Burwood Ltd., Peter, c.1935. No longer in production. Wooden. Children's puzzles.

B.V. Leisure, Unit 2, St. George's Road, Huntingdon, Cambs, PE18 6BD. 1986. Puzzles pressed by Seddons and Handley Printers. Annual catalogue produced. Cardboard puzzles including spherical globe. 3-D puzzles deleted from range in 1996, due to unsatisfactory quality? Some puzzles imported from Europe and Australia. Challenging speciality puzzles. Range of 500- 4000-piece puzzles.

C & Co., London. 1930. Out of production by World War II. Wooden. *Beryl Series.* Quite a large number survive.

Capital Series. Made by another manufacturer? c.1960s. Limited production. Cardboard. One series of famous cities.

Castile Games, Whippendale Road, Watford, Herts. WD1 7PG. 1980s and early 1990s. No longer in production. Cardboard.

Cavalcade. See Mack, W.E.

Chad Valley. Now trade name for cardboard puzzles sold by F.W. Woolworth. See Chap. 5.

Chandos Puzzles. Series name for puzzles manufactured by F.W. Warne & Co.

Cheatwell Games, Chinnor, Oxfordshire. 1994. Publisher of speciality puzzles.

Church Army, Disabled ex-Service Men's Industries, 8/12 Star Road, West Kensington, London. 1930s. Limited production. Wooden.

Cobra, Blyth & Platt Ltd., c.1930s. Cardboard. Promotional puzzle. One-off.

Condor, London. 1960s. Wooden. *Craftsman's Series.* Cut by N. Wilkes & Co. Bought by Michael Stanfield, and became part of Ravensburger group.

Conway. Tower Press Series.

Cooke Ltd., Alf, Leeds, Yorkshire. c.1920s. Limited production. Solid wooden.

Cotswood, England. 1950s - mid-1960s. Wooden. Scenic and speciality series.

Cranham Publications, Cranham Terrace, Jericho, Oxford. OX2 6DG. 1994. Cardboard. Eight designs: six Garden, two Collectors; Stamps and Railway Alphabet. Puzzles pressed by Seddons.

Crown, see Philmar.

Daily Mail Publications, Fleet Street, London. 1930s and 1940s. Cardboard. Speciality puzzles of film stars, dogs etc.

Fair quality. Probably manufactured elsewhere, perhaps by Waddington's? Boxes sometimes printed like a suitcase.

Davis Printing Co., L.R. Leicester. c.1930. Limited production? Wooden. *Winnajig* puzzles, *Fay Day Series.*

Delta, see A.V.N. Jones.

Dover Toys, England. 1920. Very limited production. Wooden.

Dubreq Ltd., 120/132 Cricklewood Lane, London, NW2 2DP. 1980s. Cardboard. Prince Charles and Princess Diana Royal Wedding souvenir.

Educa, see Robenau.

Efroc. (Corfe backwards). 1950s. Wooden. Festival of Britain puzzles.

Einco, England. 1953. Wooden. Queen Elizabeth II Coronation souvenir.

Ellar. 1945. Wooden. *The Ellar Jigsaw Puzzle.*

Ellis, William, see Welcom.

Embassy. Tower Press Series.

Emerald. Series of cardboard puzzles by Whitman.

Emerald. Series of puzzles manufactured by Jigsaws, see entry below.

En-Thrall-Us. c.1950s. No longer in production. Wooden. Children's puzzles.

Evans, W.G. Williams Mews, Stanhope Street, Euston Road, London. 1920. Limited production. Wooden. Push fit. Nursery rhymes.

Excelsior, England. c.1950. Limited production. Wooden.

Exeter, see Falcon.

Expert Puzzle, 87 Kempe Road, Kensal Rise, London, NW6. 1930s. 'Sold exclusively by Robert Plumb, ten years manager and jigsaw puzzle expert to the Graphic Gallery, Strand, London.'

Fairylite Aircraft Jigsaw. c.1945. Cardboard. Range of eight aircraft puzzles.

Falcon Games Ltd., Hatfield, Herts. See Chap. 5.

Fame. c.1970s. No longer in production. Cardboard. Railway puzzles.

Feenix Puzzles, Parsonage Road, Herne Bay, Kent. Founded 1990 by Dave and Val Cooper. Reproduction and personalised hand-cut wooden jigsaws. Makers of replacement pieces.

Fordik, England. c.1940s. Limited production. Cardboard. Nautical jigsaws.

Fortnum and Mason, 182 Piccadilly, London. 1930-c.1939. Wooden. Made elsewhere.

G.P. Genuine Jigsaws, England. c.1950s. Made by Louis Marx, *Lumar.*

Galt & Co. Ltd., James, Brookfield Road, Cheadle, Cheshire, SK8 2PN. 1980. Wooden. Children's and floor puzzles.

Gamage, A.W. London. 1930s. Solid wooden. *The Tormentum Series.*

Gee Graphite, Mirfield, Yorks. *Jigsaw Dimensions.* Speciality puzzles cut with water-jet. See Chap. 5.

Genwood Productions, England. 1940s. Limited production. Wooden.

Geographia Ltd., 55 Fleet Street, London. 1920s. Wooden. Map puzzles, probably cut elsewhere.

Gibbs Toothpaste. 1930s. Very limited edition? Two cardboard advertising puzzles, showing *Giant Decay* being repulsed from *Ivory Castles*.

Gibson's Games, Greenlea Park, Prince George's Road, London SW19 2RB. 1986. Cardboard. Speciality puzzles including *Heritage, Wildlife* and *Britain from the Air.* See Chap.5.

Glevum Series, England. 1930s. Limited production. Wooden.

Gold Box Series. Made by G. Hayter. Wooden.

Good Companion. Tower Press Series.

Good-Win. Garden series.

Graham Bros., 73, Endell Street, London WC2. c.1950s No longer in production.

Grand. Tower Press Series.

Graphic Gallery, The, 190 Strand, London. c.1950s. Wooden.

Groningen Internment Camp. 1916. One-off production. Made by men of the 1st Naval Brigade.

H.P.G. Series, England. 1940. Very limited production. Wooden.

Hamilton, James, The Bourne Centre, Southampton Road, Salisbury. See Chap. 5.

Hamley Bros. Ltd., London. 1910-25. *Society Dissected Picture Puzzle.* Coronation puzzle of HM King George V and Queen Mary. Wooden. Made elsewhere.

Handley Printers, Bredbury, Stockport, Manchester. Makers of JR Puzzles. See Chap. 5.

Harper's Novelty Toy Co. Ltd., London N7. 1915. Limited production. Wooden.

Harrods, Knightsbridge, London. c.1920s. Wooden. Made elsewhere but with Harrods' name on the box.

Harrop & Son, John, 3 Holborn Buildings, Kingsway, London. 1930s. Wooden. *Felbro Jigsaw Puzzle.*

Haven. Tower Press Series.

Hayter & Co., Gerald, Bournemouth, Dorset. Makers of Victory Wooden Puzzles. See Chap. 5.

Herald Series, see Handley Printers. Cardboard.

Hestair Puzzles, Royton, Oldham, Lancs. 1970s. Merged with Hope Puzzles. Cardboard. Wide range of traditional and children's puzzles.

Hickman, Stanley, Rose Cottage, Mill Gap, Eastbourne, Sussex. 1968. Limited production. Wooden.

Hine, Chrissie, 4 Cedar's Road, Beckenham, Kent. No longer in production. Wooden.

Historical Games and Puzzles, Leicester, England. 1993. Cardboard. Historical subjects from V. & A Museum and Tate Gallery etc.

Hobbies, Dereham, Norfolk. 1895. Leading makers of equipment for model making, including jigsaws. One puzzle, c.1940, of allied warplanes with company logo. Equipment still used commercially to cut jigsaw puzzles.

Holtzapffel & Co., London. 1900-1939. Originally an engineering company. Wooden. Unusual, challenging subjects. Retail outlet Holtzapffel & Walkers Ltd., 61 Barker Street, London W1.

Hope Puzzles. 1960s/70s. Cardboard. Merged with Hestair Puzzles.

Hopscotch U.K. Ltd., Ossett, W. Yorks. 1993. Children's giant floor puzzles.

Huvanco, Ilford, England. c.1910-1939. Wooden. Adults' puzzles, wide range of traditional subjects, catalogue lists 1000 titles.

Inghan Day. 1970s/80s. Cardboard. Adults' puzzles. Taken over by Handley Printers.

Intalok Series. See Richards Art Co., Ltd.

J.R. Jigsaws. Made by Handley Printers, Bredbury, Stockport. See Chap. 5.

J.W.S. & S. Abbreviation for J.W. Spear & Sons.

Jacques & Son, Ltd., John W. 20/21 Kirby Street, Hatton Garden, London EC1. 1930s-1939. Wooden. Country scenes.

Jerome Interlocking Jigsaw Puzzle, The, England. 1930s. Probably limited production. Wooden.

Jigsaw Puzzle, England. Pre-1941. Very limited production. Wooden.

Jones & Co., A.V.N. 64 Fore Street, London EC2. Late 1920s and 30s. Noted producer of quality wooden puzzles, contemporary of Chad Valley and Victory, similar in type and subjects. *Delta* and *South African* series among others. Some link with Chad Valley at end of company history.

K.G. Games, Kaygee House, Dallington, Northampton, NN5 7QW. 1980s. No longer in production. Cardboard. Adults' puzzles, railway series etc.

Kaleidoscope, P.O. Box 19, Swindon, Wilts, SN1 5AX. 1980s. No longer in production. Cardboard. Adults' puzzles, country scenes.

Kelly, W.R. Mill Green, Stonham Aspal, Stowmarket, Suffolk. Wooden. See Chap. 5.

Kids International Ltd., Crowthorne, Berks. 1996. Formerly L.T.I. (UK) Ltd. Cardboard. Historical and Fine Art adults' puzzles. Import Caeco Puzzles from the U.S.A.

Kipping, Miss K. E. 11 Marine Terrace, Criccieth, N.Wales. 1930s. Limited production. Hand-cut wooden.

Kolorbax, England. 1940s. Very limited production. Wooden. *Longley* series.

Kwiz Interlocking Jigsaw Puzzle, England. 1930s. Limited production.

L.G. & Co., London. 1930s/40s. Limited production. Wooden.

Leng, John, London. 1930s. Limited production. Novelty cardboard.

Lindum Puzzles, 28 Mount Street, Lincoln. 1930s. Very limited production. Wooden. Cut by H. Thornton.

Living and Learning, Abbeygate House, East Road, Cambridge. 1986. Thick cardboard. Children's puzzles imported from China.

London Geographical Institute, London. 1930s. Limited production. Wooden. Map puzzles.

London Museum Jigsaw Puzzles. 1960s. Limited production. Cardboard. *Penny Toys* and other reproduction pictures.

Longley Series, made by Kolorbax, England.

Longstaff Workshops, Robert, Appleton Road, Longworth, Oxfordshire. OX13 5EF. Wooden. Laser-cut adults and children's puzzles. See Chap. 5.

Lord Robert's Memorial Workshops for Disabled Soldiers & Sailors, Fulham, London. 1920s. Limited production? Wooden.

Luck, George, Martock, Somerset. 1980s. Wooden. Children's speciality puzzles, animal subjects and maps. Two and three layered, hand-painted puzzles.

Lumar Puzzles, trade name of Louis Marx Ltd., London. 1930s. Cardboard. Traditional subjects, fair quality. Sold through F.W. Woolworth.

Lyric Series. Produced by Tower Press.

M. & N.I. Ltd. c.1912. Very limited production. One pre-World War I wooden puzzle.

Mack, W.E. London, NW3. 1930s. Limited production. Wooden. 'Cavalcade Jigsaw Puzzle cut by British Ex-Service Men'.

Maids of Kent Craft Shop, 29 St. Margaret's Street, Canterbury, Kent. (Helen Helmore and Vera Tassell) c.1930s. Hand-cut wooden.

Magnacut puzzles. 1930s. Limited production. Wooden. Children's puzzles.

Mammoth Puzzles, The Queensway Press, 10 Great Queen Street, London W.C.2. 1930s. No longer in production. Cardboard. Large range of traditional subjects, fair quality. Prolific production.

Mandalay Jigsaw Puzzle, England. 1940. Very limited production. Wooden. Adults' puzzles.

Mandolin Puzzles, 9 Elia Street, London N1 8DE. 1985 (founded by Mrs Lalage Waldman). Cardboard. Speciality adult, including composite English scenic views. Gerard Hoffnung's *Cartoon* series.

Mansell & Co. Ltd., Vivian, Somerset. c.1950s. Limited production. Wooden. Adults' puzzles.

Mayfair Puzzles, London. c.1950. Limited production. Wooden. Adults' puzzles.

McEwen & Sons, S.M. London. 1930s-1939. Wooden. Adults' puzzles.

Mercury. Tower Press Series.

Moat House Products, Ramsey, Cambs. 1995 (founded by David Tack). Formerly Sovereign Publications. Cardboard. Speciality puzzles including railways scenes. Pressed by Seddons.

Monkey Puzzle, Norfolk, England. 1980s. No longer in production. Wooden. Hand-painted.

Mow, D.J. 16 Wadham Road, London E17. 1930. Probably very limited production. Wooden. Adults' puzzles. *Mixfix.*

Nash & Hurd, Bristol. c.1950s. Limited production. Wooden. Adults' puzzles. Scenic themes.

National Institute for the Blind, London. 1970s. Wooden. Railway locomotive with raised face for use by the blind.

National Trust, London. 1980s. Cardboard. Adults' puzzles of garden and scenic views. Probably made by another manufacturer.

New Bond Series of Jigsaw Puzzles. 1930s. Limited production. Wooden. Adults' puzzles of railway scenes.

Newington. c.1960. Cardboard. Rural scenes.

Newnes, George, see Chad Valley.

Nister, Ernest, London. c.1900-1914. Thick cardboard. Children's puzzles, contemporary scenes, airships, aeroplanes etc. Linked with Dutton of New York.

Novelty Sales Services Ltd., (N.S.S.) 10 Dane Street, London W.C.1. 1930s. Limited production. Wooden. Scenic subjects.

Nursery Rhyme, c.1960. Cardboard. Children's puzzles. Jigsaw *Selyt.*

Octorama. c.1930s. Very limited production. Wooden. English countryside.

Old English Views. 1940s? Limited production. Wooden. Adults' puzzles.

Optimago Ltd., 43 Perrymead Street, London SW6 3SN. 1980 (founded by Beverley Cohen). Hand-cut wooden. Adults' puzzles including maps, reproductions, cartoons etc. Puzzles cut by W.R. Kelly.

Orchard Toys, Debdale Lane, Keyworth, Nottingham. Founded 1969, jigsaw production began 1975. Cardboard. Children's puzzles, interchangeable pieces. Floor puzzles.

Owls of Europe Series. Made by Crown/Philmar?

Oxo advertising puzzle. 1920s. Cardboard puzzle issued to grocers.

Palitoy (General Mills U.K. Ltd.). 1960s/70s. Limited production. Cardboard. Adults' puzzles.

Patriotic Puzzles. 1915. Wooden. Probably made by Jas. Shoolbred.

Paul Lamond Games, Camden, London. 1985. Cardboard. Children's puzzles including Enid Blyton, Mystery subjects and murder mystery range. Made elsewhere.

Peacock, William, 3 Adelaide Terrace, Dame Street, London. 1860-1910. Wooden. Specialised in educational map puzzles, often double-sided. Excellent quality, solid wood puzzles in wooden, sliding-lid boxes. One of the great manufacturers, like Tuck, who launched the jigsaw puzzle industry into the twentieth century.

Pears Soap, London. c.1900-1914. Cardboard. Postcard-sized advertising puzzles for Pears soap, with famous pictures such as *Bubbles.* A pioneer in this field.

Pentaplex Ltd., Royd House, Birds Royd Lane, Brighouse, W.Yorks. Founded 1994 by Angus Lavery. *Perplexing Poultry* based on idea of Prof. Roger Penrose and also very challenging adult cardboard puzzles with repeating designs. Excellent quality pressed by another manufacturer.

Pentos Ltd. c.1960. Limited production. Cardboard. Railway scenes.

Perfect Jigsaw Puzzle, The, c.1930s. Very limited production. Wooden. Adults' puzzles.

Philmar, 51 Dace Road, London. c.1937-1980. Founded by Philip Marx. Cardboard. Large range of traditional subjects. Good quality.

Philograph Publications, North Way, Andover, Hants. 1974. Cardboard. Children's jigsaw puzzles and *Stay-put Magnetic Jigsaw* for use with magnetic baseboard.

Photocrom, London and Tunbridge Wells. 1920s/30s. No

longer in production. Wooden. Good quality puzzles from mounted photographs, railway scenes etc.

Photorama. c.1965. Cardboard. Landscapes.

Picture Puzzle Postcard, see Raphael Tuck.

Playtime Productions, Ipswich, England. 1950s. Limited production. Wooden.

Pleasure Products Ltd., Saundersness Road, London E14. c.1971. Limited production. One puzzle of Princess Anne.

Ponda, Littlehampton, Sussex. 1930s. Wooden. Children's and adults' puzzles. Thick plywood stand-up animals.

Popular Songs, 20th Century. c.1940s. Very limited production. Cardboard. Speciality puzzles. Box, shaped like a piano.

Popular Series, see Hayter.

Postcard Jigsaw Puzzles. Limited production. Cardboard. 'In aid of John Millard Memorial Women's Guild', price one penny.

Prestige Puzzles, England. 1980s. Limited production. Cardboard. Interlock series of six puzzles to make world's largest jigsaw puzzle.

Puzzleplex, Stubbs Walden, Yorks. Founded by Peter Stocken, see Chap. 5

R.N.L.I. c.1980. Cardboard puzzles of Cromer lifeboat, fund raising experiment. Made by other manufacturer.

Raphael Toys, see Handley Printers.

Ravensburger Ltd., Murdock Road, Bicester, Oxfordshire OX6 7RH. (Took over Michael Stanfield Co.) Cardboard. Good quality adults' and children's puzzles including 9000-piece, and *Wallace and Gromit*. Wide variety of titles.

Really Useful Games Ltd., 22 Tower Street, London WC2 9NS. 1994 (founded by Kevin Skinner). Cardboard sculpture range of 3-D puzzles on principle of Chad Valley *Queen Mary*, and *Bildajig*. Innovative use of cardboard sections. *The Bust, Alarm Clock* and *Globe* puzzles.

Regal Jigsaw Puzzle Company, Bexhill-on-Sea, Sussex. 1930s. Limited production. Adults', wooden puzzles.

Regency. Tower Press Series.

Rembrandt Games Ltd., Whippendell Road, Watford, Herts. (Formerly Castile Games). 1975. Wooden and cardboard.

Richard Art Co. Ltd., 40 Aldersgate Street, London EC1. 1930s. Wooden. Adults' puzzles. *Zig-Zag* and *Intalok*, ships and traditional scenes.

Robenau Toys Ltd., Abbey Road, Park Royal, London NW10 7UL. 1980s. Cardboard. Extensive range of children's and adults' puzzles up to 8000 pieces. Reproductions, scenic, wildlife and Walt Disney themes. Puzzles imported from *Educa* in Spain.

Rolark. c.1960. Cardboard. *Famous Artists* series.

Saga Puzzles, England. 1937. Limited production. Wooden.

Salmon Ltd., J, 100 London Road, Sevenoaks, Kent TN13 IBB. 1920. Jigsaw production ended in 1955. Wooden and cardboard. Makers of *Academy Series* of puzzles. Wide range of traditional subjects for adults and children, size range from 50 - 1500 pieces. Significant production though not as prolific as Chad Valley or Victory (see Chap.5).

Sanderson, H.A. 14 East Holm, Letchworth, Herts. 1930s. Limited production. Wooden.

Sceptre. Tower Press Series.

Scottish Toys, Glasgow, Scotland. 1930s. Limited production. *Bildajig* 3-D wooden puzzle boats. Three models only.

Seddon Packaging and Printing, Northampton. 1990s. Cardboard. Manufacturers but not publishers of puzzles (see Chap.5).

Shaw & Co. Ltd., A.B. 3 Creed Lane, London EC4. 1930s/40s. Probably limited production. Wooden. Ship subjects.

Shaw's 'Matchless' Jigsaw Puzzles, from Butlers, East Oxford Shopping Centre, 167 Cowley Road, Oxford. 1930s. Cardboard.

Shoolbred & Co., Jas, Tottenham House, Tottenham Court Road, London. c.1910. Limited production. Solid wood. Rural and traditional scenes.

Simkin & Marshall Ltd., London. c.1940. Limited production. Wooden. *Hall Court* and *Pip, Squeak & Wilfred* series of puzzles.

Smith, Miss E. Balconas Cottage, Charlton Kings, Cheltenham. 1930s. Limited production. Wooden. 'Puzzles made for the benefit of the Universities Mission to Central Africa'.

Smith, W.H. Puzzles specially made by Chad Valley, 1930s, and cardboard puzzle collection. Wooden.

Snowies, England. 1930s. Very limited production. Wooden.

South London Libraries. 1930s. Wooden, large. Rural scenes.

Sovereign Publications, St. Ives and Ramsey, Cambs. 1983-1993. Cardboard. Railway scenes etc. Pressed by Seddons. Now Moathouse Products.

Spears Games, Wokingham, Berks. 1995. Cardboard. Adults' and children's speciality puzzles.

Spear & Son. J.W. Enfield, Middlesex, England, and Bavaria. 1878. Hand-cut thick cardboard. Children's puzzles 1900-1935. Took over G. Hayter in 1970 and continued production of the wooden *Gold Box* series until 1988. Puzzle making equipment was then sold to Michael Stanfield Ltd.

Stanfield Ltd., Michael, Murdock Road, Bicester, Oxfordshire. 1959-1990. Wooden and cardboard. Children's and adults' puzzles. *Master Craftsman* series. Extensive range. Taken over by Ravensburger in 1990.

Stocken, Peter, Puzzleplex, see Chap. 5.

Strome & Co., 92 Victoria Street, London SW1. c.1930s. Limited production. Wooden.

Studio Picture Puzzle, London. 1920. Very limited production. Wooden. Sold in Cheapside.

Suffolk Art Puzzles. 1920s. Limited production. Wooden. Puzzles cut and finished by ex-servicemen.

T.P. Series, England. 1940. Wooden. Probably Tower Press.

Tate Gallery. Waddington Series.

Tate Gallery Pocket Puzzle, London. 1979. Limited production. Cardboard. Gallery picture reproductions.

Terminus. Tower Press Series.

Thames Engraving. No information.

Thornton Ltd., H, 28 Mount Street, Lincoln. 1910-1920. Limited production. Wooden.

Timpo Jigsaw Puzzles, Timpo Toys, England. 1950s. Thick plywood. London scenes.

Toby Toys, England. 1960s. Cardboard. Military series.

Tomahawk Toys, Hemyock, Devon. 1987 (founded by David Hawkins). Wooden scroll puzzles.

Tonair Products Ltd., 35 Dale Street, Manchester. 1969. Founded by Tony Eccles. Cardboard. Speciality puzzles.

Topsail Productions, England. 1960s. Limited production. Cardboard. Traditional subjects.

Tower Press, Wales and London. Makers of *Good Companions* and around twelve other series. See Chap. 5.

Town and Country. Probably a series title. Cardboard.

Trigsaws, Half Acre, Highland Road, Taverham, Norwich NR8 6QP. 1988 (founded by Martin Smith). Hand-cut, multi-layer wooden. Wide range of products.

Trowsdale & Son., W.J. Alfreton, Derbyshire. See Chap. 5.

Tru-Cut. Probably a series title. Cardboard.

Tru-View. Probably a series title. Cardboard.

Tuck, Raphael, London. Very important twentieth-century manufacturer. Wooden. See Chap. 5.

Uncle Mack's Jigsaw Puzzle. 1930s/40s. Probably limited production. Wooden. Cut by British ex-servicemen.

Union Jack Jigsaw. The, c.1950s. Very limited production. Wooden. Rural scenes.

V.T.H. Puzzles, England. 1920s/30s. Limited production. Wooden.

Valentine & Sons, Kinnowel Road, Dundee, Scotland. c.1935-c.1970. Limited production. Wooden. Traditional subjects, ships and boats. Puzzles were a sideline.

Valiant, see Hestair/Hope.

Valour. Tower Press Series.

Veltoy, England. c.1930/40. Limited production. Wooden. Map subjects.

Victory. Trade name of G. Hayter, most significant maker of wooden puzzles. See Chap. 5.

Voyager. Tower Press Series.

W.P. & S., London. c.1915/20. Limited production. Wooden. *Playtime Picture Puzzle.*

Waddington, John - Waddington Games Ltd., Leeds, Yorkshire. c.1935-1997. Leading manufacturer of cardboard puzzles. See Chap. 5.

Walmer. Tower Press Series.

Warne & Co., F, Bedford Court, Bedford Street, Strand, London. 1920s/30s. Wooden. *Chandos* series including traditional subjects and Beatrix Potter. Also *Bedford* series. Quite a prolific producer though puzzles were a sideline.

Welcom. 1930s. Chad Valley Series?

Wellington Toys, Great Harwood, Lancs. c.1920. Limited production. Wooden, one of Buckingham Palace.

Wentworth Wooden Jigsaw Puzzle Co. Ltd., The Dairy Farm, Pinkney Park, Malmesbury, Wilts SN16 0NX. 1994 (founded by Kevin Preston). Wooden. Laser-cut adults' puzzles. See Chap. 5.

White, Sarah, Briff, Briff Lane, Bucklebury, Berks RG7 6SN. 1981. Hand-cut wooden. Challenging and high-quality personalised puzzles.

Whitman Publishing, a Pentos Company, London. 1970-c.1990. Cardboard. 500- to 1000-piece puzzles of traditional subjects, foreign scenes. Quite prolific production.

Wilces Premier Jigsaw Puzzle, Wilces Toyshops Ltd., 8/10 High Street, Arcock, Cardiff, Wales. c.1920. Limited production. Wooden.

Wild Geese Workshop, Belfast, N. Ireland. 1980s. Limited production. Cardboard. Fiendishly difficult *Stone Wall Puzzle*.

Wilkes & Co., N. London. 1950s. Cutter of wooden puzzles. See Tower Press Co., Chap. 5.

Willis Toys Ltd., Debden Road, Newport, Saffron Walden, Essex CB11 3RY. 1980s. Wooden. Children's puzzles cut by W.R. Kelly. Speciality and traditional subjects.

Wilton Puzzles. Probably series name. c.1950. Wooden.

Winfield 'Crown' Series. c.1970. Cardboard.

Woolworth, F.W., London & branches. Commissioned puzzles from Mammoth, 1930s and now Chad Valley name, 1990s.

Workshop For The Blind, Miss D.V. Purvis, 104 Westcombe Park Road, Blackheath, London. 1930s. Limited production. Wooden.

Wyndham, see Arrow Games.

Zag-Zaw. Series name of main Raphael Tuck series of wooden puzzles.

Zig-Zag Puzzle Co. The, Carlton Street, London. 1910s/20s. Wooden. Traditional countryside scenes.

BIBLIOGRAPHY

Beves, Carolyn, *The British Jigsaw Puzzle Library* Leamington Spa, 1993
Bekkering, Betsy & Geert, *Piece by Piece* Holland, 1988
Brearley, H.D., *A History of Waddingtons* Waddington Games, c.1985
Hannas, Linda, *The English Jigsaw Puzzle, 1760-1890* Wayland Publishers, London, 1972
Hannas, Linda, *The Jigsaw Puzzle Book* Hutchinson & Co., 1981
London Museum, The, *200 Years of Jigsaw Puzzles* 1968
Price, Brian, *Victory – A Family Concern* Privately published thesis, Nov. 1996
Ray, Charles, (ed) *The Romance of the Nation* The Educational Book Co. Ltd., London, 1930
Trevelyan, G.M., *English Social History* Longmans, 1942
Whitely, F.M., *Collectors Gazette*, 'Jigsaw Puzzles, the Next Collectable' June, 1991
Whitely, F.M., & Tyler, T.M., *The Chad Valley Promotional Puzzles* Magic Fairy Publishing, 1990
Williams, Anne, *Cutting a Fine Figure: The Art of the Jigsaw Puzzle* Museum of our National Heritage, Lexington, Mass. U.S.A. 1996
Williams, Anne, *Jigsaw Puzzles* Wallace Homestead Book Co., U.S.A., 1990

INDEX

The index relates to the black and white section of the book.

A
A.1. Puzzle Club, London, 39, 125
Academy Series, see Salmon
Adby, Peter, 32, 33
adhesives, 18. 19. 22, 37
Adydos Ltd., 125
Allen Ltd., Ian, 125
amateur puzzles, 19, 20, 23, 37-38
Andrews, E.J., 26
Archers Jigsaws, 125
Armitage Bros., Ltd., 125
Armstrong, Mark, 37, 40
Army & Navy Stores, 125
Arrow Games, 32, 125
Arrow Games Series, see Arrow
Arty-Zan, 125
Arthur Park, 11
Ashley Puzzles, 125
Associated Newspapers Ltd., 125
Attlee, Lord, 40
Attwell, Mabel Lucie, 24
auctions, 15, 24, 25
Austin, Ann,. 125
Austin Project Marketing Ltd., 125

B
B.V. Leisure, 42, 126
Bacon & Co., G.W., 125
Baker & Co., John, 125
Baldwin, Elsie, 39, 40
Ballad of John Gilipin, The, 9
Barfoots, 11
Beales Store, 28
Bear, Bear & Bear Ltd., 125
Beaux Arts, 125
Beaverbrook Newspapers, 125
Bedford Series, 125
Belinda, 125
Bellow & Higden, 125
Benevolent Confraternity of
  Dissectologists, The, 15, 41
Benson, Sid, 30
Bentalls Store Ltd., 125
Beraton, 125
Berry, Mary, 125
Beryl Series, 125
Betts, John, 11
Beverley, 125
Beves, Carolyn, 39, 40
Big Jigs, 42, 125
Big Top Puzzle, 125
Big Value Jigsaw Puzzle, 125
Bildajig, 125
Bon Marche, 125
Bond, E.E., 126
Bond, Eric, 37, 40
Bonzo, 26
Boots The Chemist, 27, 32, 126
boxes, 10-12, 20-21, 24, 26, 28-34, 40

Breckon, Don, 31
British Beauty Spots, 126
British Home Stores, 32,
British India Steamship Co., 25, 27
British Isles Jigsaw Map, 126
British Jigsaw Puzzle Club, 15, 37, 39
British Jigsaw Puzzle Library, 40, 41
British Legion Poppy Factory, 126
British Printing Corporation, 26
Bulmer's Cider Co. Ltd., 126
Burwood Ltd., Peter, 126

C
C. & Co., 126
Cadbury, 34
Caerphilly Castle, 34
Capital Series, 126
car boot sales, 15
cardboard puzzles, 9-10, 14, 18,
  22-25, 27, 29-30, 33, 34, 42
Carpenter, Nicholas, 11
Castile Games, 42, 126
Cavalcade, 126
Chad Valley 14, 17-18, 21, 23-27,
  30, 33, 39, 126,
Chandos Puzzles, 39, 126
Cheatwell Games, 42, 126
*Chronological Tables of English History
for the Instruction of Youth,* 11
Church Army, 126
Cobra, 126
Collectors' Gazette, The, 15
Collectors' Roundabout, 41
colour prints, 18
Conan Doyle, Sir Arthur, 26
Condor, 32, 126
Conway, 126
Cooke Ltd., 126
Cooper, Dave, 10, 43
Cooper, Val, 20, 43
'collectables', 15, 23, 26, 34
commissioned artists, 33-36
commissioned puzzles, 14, 19
computer technology, 22, 23, 34, 43
constructional puzzles, 29,
Cotswood, 126
Country Life, 37
Cowper, William, 9
Craig, James, The Hon, 39
Cranham Publications, 42, 126
Crompton, Pearl & Michael, 40
Crossland Cutters, 34
Crown, 126
Crutchley, 11
Cunard White Star, 14, 25, 27, 31
Cuneo, Terence, 31, 37
cutting, 9, 10, 37, 38

D
Daily Mail Publications, 126
Darton, William, 9, 11
Davis Printing Co, Ltd., L.R., 126
Delta, 126
Depression, The, 14, 23, 27, 30
Dickens, Charles, 28
dissected maps and puzzles, 9, 11, 41
double-sided puzzles, 11, 38
Dover Toys, 126
Dubreq Ltd., 126
Dunlop, 14, 25, 27

E
Early Learning Centre, The, 42
East Anglian Puzzle Club, 39
educational, 9-13, 28-29, 35, 43
Educa, 126
Edward VII, 13
Efroc, 126
Ehrlich, Hans, 31-32
Einco, 126
electric jigsaw, 19, 20, 38
Ellar, 126
Ellis William, 126
Embassy by Whitman, 126
Emerald, 126
English Jigsaw Puzzle 1760-1890, 9
En-Thrall-Us, 126
Esterman, Alfred, 32
Everybody's Magazine, 31
Evans, W.G., 126
Exchange and Mart, The, 15
Excelsior, 126
Exeter, 126
Expert Puzzle, 126

F
Fairylite Aircraft Jigsaw, 126
Falcon Games, 25, 33, 42, 126
Fame, 126
Feenix Puzzles, 126
Fine Art Developments, 26
First World War, 13, 21, 23, 27
Ford Motor Co., 21, 37
Fordham Factory, 31
Fordik, 126
form-making, 19
Fortnum & Mason, 126
fretsaw, 9-10, 14, 16, 27, 36-37
Frith, W.P., 23
Fry's, 34
Fryer, George, 32

G
G.P. Genuine Jigsaws, 126
Gall & Inglis, 11
Galt & Co. J., 35, 42, 126
Gamage, A.W., 126
Gasmans of Dagenham, 32, 126

Gee, Colin, 21, 22, 34, 43
Gee Graphite Ltd., 21, 34, 35, 126
Gee, Pauline, 21, 34
Gell, Phillip, 36
General Mills, 27
Genwood Productions, 126
Geographia Ltd., 126
Gibbs Toothpaste, 127
Gibson Games. 34, 42, 127
Gibson Games Series, 34,
Giles cartoons, 15
Glevum Series, 127
Gold Box Series, see Victory
Golden Gate Products, 125
Good Companions Series, 127
Good-Win Series, 127
Graham Bros., 127
Grand, 127
Graphic Gallery, The, 127
G.W.R., 14-15, 23-25, 27, 30
Groningen Internment Camp, 127
guide pictures, 12, 14, 28, 33

H
H.P.G. Series, 127
half-puzzles, 17, 32
Hamilton, James, 36, 42, 127
Hamley Bros., 127
Handley Printers, 34, 42, 127
Hannas, Linda, 9, 11, 24
Harper's Novelty Toy Co. Ltd., 127
Harrods, 127
Harrop & Son, John, 127
Hasbro, 27, 42,
Hausemann and Hotte, 33
Haven, 127
Hayter, G.H., 14, 26-30, 38-39, 127
Hawks Technical and Bobst, 19, 34
Hegner saw, 38
Helmore, Helen, 44
Henderson, John, 9
Herald Series, 127
Hestair Puzzles, 127
Hickman, Stanley, 127
Hine, Chrissie, 127
Historical Games and Puzzles, 42, 127
Hobbies of Dereham, 17, 35, 38, 127
Holtzapffel & Co., 25, 39, 127
Hope Puzzles, 127
Hopscotch U.K. Ltd., 127
Hunt, Holman, 26
Hurst, Ted, 33
Huvanco Puzzles, 127

I
Ingan Day, 127
Intalok Series, 127
Inspector Hornleigh Series, see
  Waddington

interchangeable pieces, 22, 35, 43
Isle of Wight Jigsaw Festival, 44
Izzard, James, 11

J
J.R. Puzzles, see Handley
J.W.S. & S. 127
Jacques & Son, Ltd., 127
Jeffery, John, 9
Jefferys, Thomas, 9
Jerome Interlocking Jigsaw Puzzle,
  127
Jigsaw Dimensions, 22
jigsaw, 19, 20-22
Jigsaw Puzzle, 127
Jigsaw Puzzle Libraries and Clubs,
  39-41
Johnson, Alfred, 27
Johnson, Andrew, 26
Johnson, Joseph, 27
Johnson Bros., 27
Jondorf, Harry, 31, 33
Jondorf, Wilhelm, 31
Jones & Co., A.V.N., 25, 127
Jones, Goldwynne, 40
Jones, Kitty, 40
Jones, Nancy, 40
Jones, Robert,40
Jumbo, 42

K
K.G. Games, 127
Kaleidoscope, 127
Kelly, W.A., 36, 42, 127
Kershaw, Andrew, 39
Kids International Ltd., 127
King George V locomotive, 17
Kipping, Miss K.E., 127
Kolorbax, 127
Kwiz Interlocking Jigsaw Puzzle, 127

L
L. G. & Co., 127
Langfords, Birmingham, 32
'largest' puzzle, 21
laser-cutting, 20-23, 35-36, 42, 43
Lawrence, Rachael, 39
Lea, Mr., 40
Leng, John, 127
Lindum Puzzles, 127
Lines Bros., 32
Lines, Moray, 32
Living and Learning, 127
London Geographical Institute, 127
London Museum Jigsaw Puzzles, 128
Longley Series, 128
Longstaff, Robert, 22, 35, 42, 128
Longstaff, Yvonne, 35
Lord Roberts, 128
Lost in Transit, 24
Luck, George, 36, 42, 128
Luck, Kay, 36
Lumar Puzzles, 128
Lyric Series, 128

M
M.D.F. board, 22, 35, 37
M. & N.I. Ltd., 128
Mack, W.E., 128
MacDougall, Dolly, 39
MacMillan, Dorothy, 40
Maids of Kent Craft Shop, 44, 128
Magnacut Puzzles, 128
mail order, 34, 39
Mammoth Puzzles, 128
Mandalay Jigsaw Puzzle, 128
Mandolin Puzzles, 42, 128
Manders, Christine, 41
Mansell & Co. Ltd., 128
maps, 11-13, 28, 30-31, 34
Marx, Louis, 30
Mayfair Puzzles, 128
McEwen & Sons Ltd., 128
Mercury, 128
micro puzzle, 38

Millennium Falcon, 22
Miller, Fred, 32
Milton Bradley, 32, 33, 42
Misfits, 10
Miss Rutherford's Puzzle Club, 39
Monopoly, 15, 30, 42
Moat House Products, 42, 128
Monkey Puzzle, 128
Mow, D.J., 128
Murder She Wrote, 30

N
Nash & Hurd, 128
National Institute for the Blind, 128
National Trust, The, 36, 128
New Bond Series, 128
Newington, 128
Newnes, George, 128
Nister, Ernest, 128
Norton, Alison, 20
Novelty Sales Services Ltd., 128
Nursery Rhyme, 128

O
Octorama, 128
Old English Views, 128
Optimago Puzzles, 23, 43, 128
Orchard Toys, 42, 128
Original Jigsaw Puzzle Club, 39
Owls of Europe Series, 128
Oxo, 128

P
Palitoy, 27, 128
Parkers Bros. USA., 30
Patriotic Puzzles, 128
Paul Lamond Games, 42, 127
Peacock, Willliam, 11, 13, 27, 128
Peacock's Superior Dissection, 11
Pears Soap, 128
Pedley, Eric, 37, 40
Pedley, Ray, 37, 40
Pentaplex Ltd., 128
Pentos Ltd., 128
Perfect Jigsaw Puzzle, The, 128
Philip & Son, 11
Philmar, 128
Philograph Publications, 128
Photocrom, 129
Photorama, 129
Picture Puzzle Postcard, 129
plastic, 42
Playtime Productions, 129
Pleasure Products Ltd., 129
Pleasure Toys, 42
plywood, 9-10, 14, 18-19, 27-28,
  35, 37
Ponda, 129
Popular Series, 129
Popular Songs, 129
Postcard Jigsaw Puzzles, 129
Prestige Puzzles, 129
Preston, Kevin, 35
Prince Charles, 31
Princess Diana, 31
Princess Helena Victoria, 40
Princess Marie Louise, 40
printing presses, 19, 22, 27, 31-34
production records, 15, 24, 38, 43
promotional puzzles, 11, 21, 25, 27
Punch, 14
Purnell & Sons, 26
puzzle postcard, 26, 28
Puzzleplex, 34, 43, 129

Q
Queen Elizabeth II, 29, 40
Queen Elizabeth, 29,
Queen Mary, 15, 29, 33
Queen Victoria, 13, 26

R
R.N. L.I., 129
R.S.P.B., 36
Raphael Toys, 129
Ravensburger Ltd., 32, 42, 129

Really Useful Games, 42, 129
Regal Jigsaw Puzzle Co., 129
Regency, 129
Rembrandt Games Ltd., 42, 129
replacement pieces, 20-21
Richard Art Co. Ltd., 129
Richardson, Steve, 22
Robenau Toys, 42, 129
Rolark, 129
Royal Academy, 11
Royal Family, 27

S
Saalheimer, Bernard, 31-32
Saga Puzzles, 129
Salmon & Co, J., 25, 28, 33, 129
Salmon, Derek, 33
Salmon Series, 33
Sanderson, HA., 129
Sawbridge, Dick, 37, 40
Sceptre, 129
Scottish Toys, 129
Second World War, 18, 21, 23, 27,
  29, 30, 33
Seddon Packaging & Printing, 33,
  42, 129
Shaw & Co. Ltd., A.B., 129
Shaw's 'Matchless' Jigsaw
  Puzzles, 129
Shoolbred & Co., Jas., 129
Simkin & Marshall Ltd., 129
'smallest' puzzle, 21
Smith, Miss E, 129
Snowies, 129
South London Libraries, 129
Sovereign Publications, 129
Spear & Son, J.E., 29-30, 129
Spears Games, 25, 27, 125
Spilsbury, John, 9, 11, 42
Spooner, William, 11
Spurling, J., 26
stack-cutting, 17, 20, 23, 36
Stanfield Ltd., Michael, 32, 129
Stave Jigsaw Puzzles, 22, 34
Stocken, Enid, 34, 37, 40
Stocken, Jonathan, 43
Stocken, Peter, 22, 34, 43, 129
Stokes, Peter, 37, 40
Strome & Co., 129
Stroud, John, 29
Studdy, G.E., 26
Studio Picture Puzzle, 129
Suffolk Art Puzzles, 129
Swinbourne Johnson, Roger, 27

T
3-D Puzz, 31, 42
T.P. Series, 129
tablemat puzzles, 22, 35
Taggart, 30
Tassell, Vera, 44
Tate Gallery, 130
television and radio, 15, 30
Terminus, 130
Thames Engraving, 130
Thematic Series, see Victory
Thornton Ltd., H., 130
three-dimensional, 22, 34
Timpo Jigsaw Puzzles, 130
Toby Toys, 130
Tomahawk, 42, 130
Tonair Products Ltd., 130
Topical Series, see Victory
Topsail Productions, 130
Tower Press, 18, 24, 31-33, 130
Tower Press Series, 31, 32, 33
Town and Country, 130
Toys-R-Us, 33
treadle-jigsaw, 9-10, 16, 19, 22-23,
  33-34, 37-38
Trigsaws, 130
Trowsdale & Son, W.J., 33, 35-36,
  42, 130

Tru-Cut, 130
Tru-View, 130
Trup, Julius, 32
Truth, 26
Tuck, Desmond, 26
Tuck, Raphael, 11-12, 13, 21,
  25-26, 37, 29, 130
Turner, J.M.W., 26

U
Uncle Mack's Jigsaw Puzzle, 130
Union Jack Jigsaw, 130
United Oversea, 27

V
V.T.H. Puzzles, 130
Valentine & Sons, 130
Valiant, 130
Valour, 130
value of jigsaw puzzles, 23-25
Van Riebeeck, Johann, 14
Veltoy, 130
Vibro jigsaw, 38
Victory, 14, 25-26, 28-30, 33,
  37-40, 130
Victory Series, 28, 29, 30
Voyager, 130

W
W.H.,Smith & Sons, 27, 32, 129
W.P. & S., London, 130
Waddington Games, 130
Waddington, John, 18-19, 21-22,
  24, 30-32, 34, 42, 130
Waddington's Circular Puzzles, see
  Waddington.
Waddington's Giant Jigsaw, 30
Walmer, 130
Walt Disney, 25, 31
Wallis Snr, John, 9, 11
Wallis, Edward, 11
Wallis, John, 11
Warne & Co., F., 130
Washington Capitol Building, 22
Waterfield, Kitty, 40
water-jet cutting, 21-23, 34, 43
Watson, Norman, 30
Welcom, 130
Wellington Toys, 130
Wentworth Wooden Jigsaw Co.
  Ltd., 35, 43, 130
whimsies, 12, 26, 28, 34-35, 37-38
White, Paul, 38
White, Sara, 23, 37-38, 40, 43, 130
Whitehead, Mrs, 40
Whitman Publishing, 130
Wilces Premier Jigsaw Puzzle, 130
Wild Geese Workshop, 130
Wilkes & Co., N., 32, 130
Wills Scheme, 30
Willis Toys, 36, 42, 130
Wilton Puzzles, 130
Winfield 'Crown' Series, 130
wooden puzzles, 12, 16, 18-19,
  22-27, 29, 33, 35-36, 39-42
Woolworth, 14, 30, 32,130
Workshop for the Blind, 130
World Wildlife Fund, The, 36
Worsfold, Meredith, 37-38, 40
Wyndham, 130

Z
Zag-Zaw,130
Zig-Zag Puzzle Co., 130

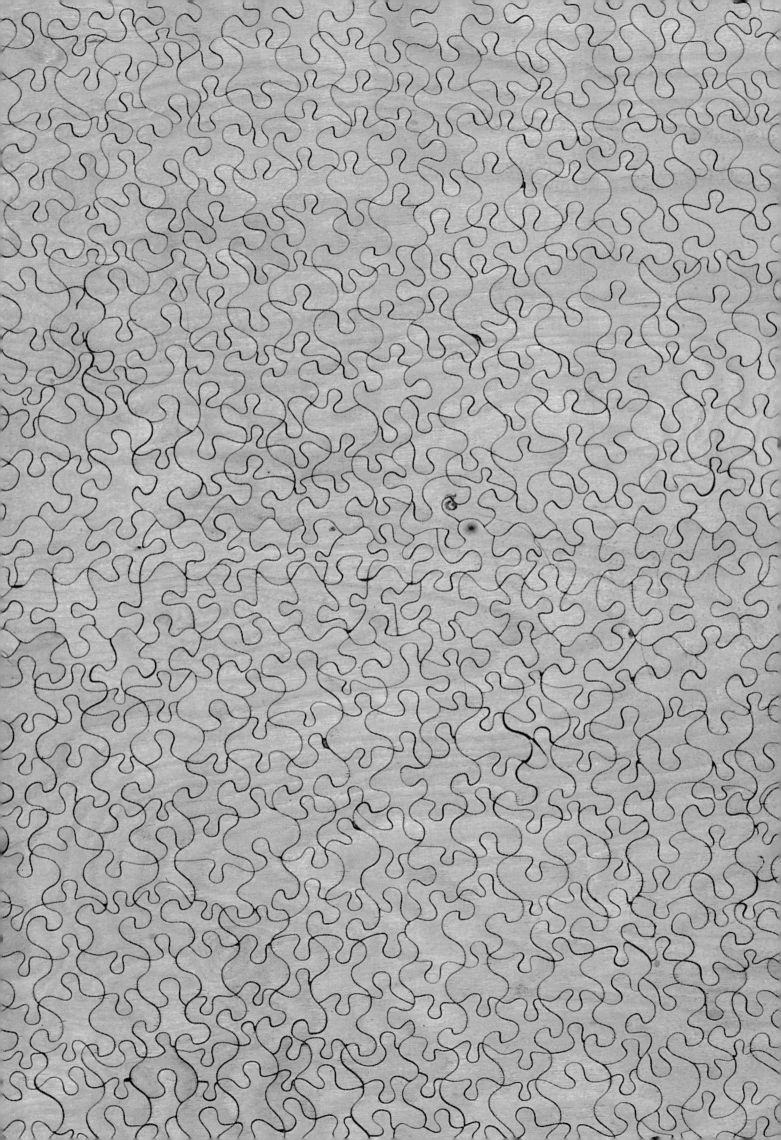